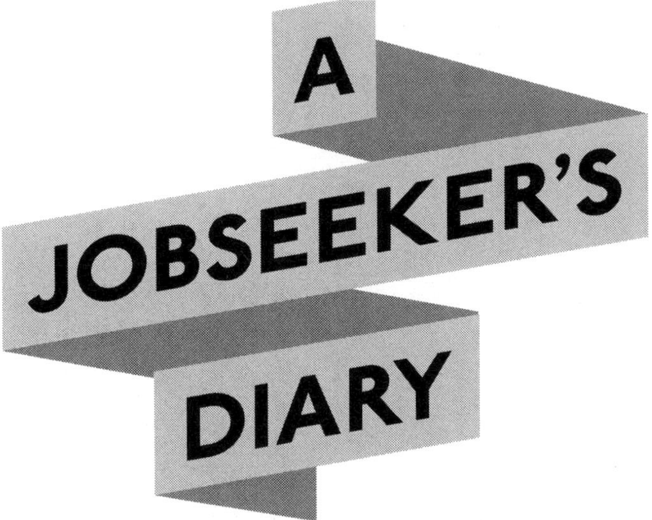

Unlocking Employment Secrets

Dr. Fawzi Abou-Chahine

First published in 2021
by Chahine Communications Ltd

ISBN 978-1-5272-8908-6

Editor: Rebecca Bush

Designer: Kathryn Corlett

Table of Contents

Preface

The vast majority of UK, EU and USA postgraduates and PhD holders leave academic employment for industry roles. Census data in both the USA and the UK indicates that this demographic of degree- and doctorate-level individuals has doubled to 4.5 million in the past twenty years[1]. Moreover, in the decade between the last economic downturn in 2010 and the one in 2020[2], the number of researchers in the EU increased from approximately 1.5 to 2 million, almost half of whom now work within commercial sectors rather than in traditional academic positions. Of those who move to industry, roughly half change profession entirely, with a higher proportion of postgraduates in social sciences leaving for industry, compared to their physical science peers[3]. The principal reason for this migration to industry is relatively straightforward: the supply of tertiary-educated employees looking for employment in academia significantly outweighs the demand. Of the relatively few positions that are available, they are typically located in another city or country, and will be in the form of a fixed term contract on a comparatively lower salary than in the commercial sector. The result is a net transition to the seemingly more stable jobs in industry, in pursuit of greater financial security. These socio-economic pressures also result in a higher proportion of female postgraduates and ethnic minority groups leaving academia. This is part of why academia has a diversity problem – but this isn't the book to open that particular can of worms!

As someone who has gone through such a career transition, I recognised that I was initially unprepared for the fundamentally different reality of employment in the commercial sector. I also struggled to find career advice that was aimed at someone like me – much of what I found was aimed at school leavers and graduates, and was honestly pretty generic. So this is the book I wish I had had. It started life as brief, unconnected notes in a diary, recording my slow struggle to find employment. However, after recording and analysing my mistakes, I was soon able to develop a more successful approach that helped me step back into fulfilling employment in industry, and slowly address my mental health difficulties. After a successful career progression, we have A Jobseeker's Diary, a nonfiction narrative that presents helpful career guidance and mental health advice amid a candid account of my efforts to overcome unemployment, and develop a successful career following a transition from academia to industry.

---

1   www.census.gov/library/stories/2019/02/number-of-people-with-masters-and-phd-degrees-double-since-2000.html
2   ec.europa.eu/eurostat/statistics-explained/index.php/R_%26_D_personnel
3   www.hepi.ac.uk/2020/02/17/the-employment-of-phd-graduates-in-the-uk-what-do-we-know

I dedicate this book to anyone who is going through the difficulties of jobseeking or unemployment. You are not alone, and you will succeed.

Introduction: My story

In January 2015, my fixed-term contract as a researcher at Tampere University of Technology, Finland, expired, and I was left wondering what to do next with my life. What job outside of academia could I do, and where could I find it? I had lived in Finland for only a year, having initially moved there after being unable to find a suitable next role in the UK, where I had completed my doctorate. And I'm not the only one to have faced this challenge. So many friends and colleagues I've spoken to over the years tell me of their own battles to find employment in academia: how they are tired of relocating from city to city, or country to country; tired of the endless fixed term contracts with scarce opportunities of a raise; and tired of the seemingly absent jobs available to them. You may be feeling the same way!

So, there I was in Finland, waiting for inspiration to strike. As the winter snow continued to descend outside, I slowly packed my bags to return home, and began to realise that I had grown tired of the academic lifestyle. Instead of a fulfilling life of research, academic challenge, and intellectual growth, it seemed to have become a Sisyphean nightmare of endlessly applying for fixed-term contracts, intellectual snobbery, and typically low wages compared to industry. So I decided to enjoy the next few months travelling, casually spending the modest savings I had amassed, while I considered what I could possibly do instead. I had convinced myself I would get inspiration along the way. Three months later, I was low on funds and inspiration, and was nowhere closer to an answer of what I could do, or even wanted to do. I knew I had to return to the real world soon; I was beginning to get anxious.

As luck would have it, on a flight home I became friendly with the passenger next to me. She worked as a recruitment consultant in "Executive Search" she said, and I nodded along politely trying to work out what that meant. "I find staffing solutions for premium clients, and I focus in the university sector. I'm actually looking to fill in a senior research post in London," she explained, as I tried to decipher 'staffing solutions' and 'premium clients'. "The problem is, these candidates only respond well to other academics, so we often need to employ former research staff or ex-PhDs to develop relationships with them. You don't know any do you?"

My grin grew wider as I slowly realised the opportunity that developed before me. "Maybe you should hire me," I blurted nervously. "I'm an academic and looking for a job." My forwardness was surprisingly well received, and I was invited to a formal interview three weeks later.

I would love, at this point, to tell you that I got the job and everyone lived happily ever after… but sadly, that could not be further from the truth. I remember entering the interview with a misplaced sense of confidence, perhaps even an arrogance, that I now realise the interviewer was quick to notice. I had surely answered all the questions well, and I was certain I was smart enough. However, my application was unsuccessful. I had the ability, the competence, and the intelligence that the role required, but I did not have the right attitude. At the time, I did not understand what this meant, because within the academic bubble, researchers are trained to value knowledge and intellect among the most prized assets, while personality or attitude is irrelevant if you can perform the role. However, I was beginning to realise that this was not the case in the very different world of industry. I was about to discover how truly different it was, the hard way.

The bubble well and truly burst, so began my crash-landing to reality. I had run out of money and returned to live at home. Despite the relative privilege of being able to live rent-free with family – something I am aware that not everyone can do – the loss of financial independence dealt a further blow to my confidence. I scrambled to reassess what possible capability I had to offer the working world. I did not have any relevant skills at all, or so I thought. Sure, I could fix a broken laser, oversee several concurrent experiments, and teach students complicated concepts, but I had convinced myself that these were not valued in most industries, except perhaps high-technology sectors or contract research organisations. As a result, I was too narrow minded in my jobsearch, focusing only on applying for positions where, I thought, my specific scientific knowledge was necessary. Ironically, despite all the knowledge I had, I was too ignorant to see the value in highlighting how transferable my experience and skills were, and describing them in the commercial language that the business world speaks. As a result, these applications were all unsuccessful.

After a while, I tried to cast the net wider and apply for positions where a basic knowledge of science was useful. I did not understand it at the time, but these also failed because I was not able to sell myself and my relevant skills in the necessary way. With every further rejected application, my self-doubt grew more concentrated, until it slowly dissolved my ego. While friends enjoyed the summer sunshine, I lingered indoors, continually applying for jobs like an automaton, never succeeding but never stopping either, as it did not occur to me that my approach was incorrect.

My Story

Eventually, I tried applying for almost anything and everything, and of course so many of these positions were clearly unsuitable for me for many reasons. However, at the time, I was in such a disengaged mental state that I did not realise this, and my only conclusion was that I was repeatedly being rejected because I was not good enough.

Soon the autumnal months ushered the daylight away and my appetite faded as the depression set in. If happiness is a warm embrace, then I was in possession of a seemingly endless chill. I had lost count of how many job applications I had submitted since I first started my jobsearch and I could not understand why I was failing, or why I had been so unemployable. I had bought and read several books written by career gurus on how to get a job and tried to follow them religiously, but it still wasn't clicking for me. Invariably, I found myself skimming endless streams of highly repetitive internet articles on employment tips, often well into the night. But staring at a computer to read annoyingly upbeat and often poorly written content when you've spent an entire day at the computer writing did not help my fragile mental state.

One thing you do learn from academia is the practice of reflection and analysis. In almost all higher education, not least the sciences, it is crucial to look at what has been done and reflect on or critique it – you learn from your errors and the work of others. So, at this lowest of low points is when I decided to keep a diary, to record all the helpful pieces of information I had learnt from the resources that were available. I also reviewed several previous job applications I had written to try to identify where I had been going wrong. Slowly but surely, I began to amass a growing collection of mistakes I had made and tips on how to improve. And with each new written application, I became gradually more confident, which enhanced the quality of the applications. By mid-November, I had written five new job applications and as the last month of the year dawned, I received three invitations to interview. The embers within burst back into flames; I blew a sigh of relief.

As the end of the year drew quickly forward, and the interviews approached even faster, I continued in a state of bemusement. I went into each interview mentally prepared, with my heart filled with hope and humility. In a twist of fortune, in January 2016, I had received three offers from all three interviews. Almost a year after my distressing unemployment journey had started, I was in the unprecedented position of having the ability to choose where I wanted my first step in a new career to go. Marketing? Sales? Finance? My bemusement turned to shock; I had broken the curse.

The next few months were the happiest days I could remember in a long time. I had an income, I had a company shirt, I had a work schedule, I had structure to my day, I had a reason to leave the house, I had an excuse to jump out of bed in the morning... in short, I was ecstatic! Over the next few years, I decided to write up the notes I had made in the diary I had kept, to serve as a reminder to the future me. A reminder that I was once too proud, how a know-it-all knew nothing, but also how I overcame an abyss of failure. As I slowly progressed up the career ladder, I embraced every opportunity to learn new things about the world of industry, to strengthen my capabilities, and develop as many new ones as I could. I iteratively added new lessons I learned in my diary should I ever need to recollect them.

This book is the result of that diary. Although I have taken the chance to review and update it with new knowledge that I've learned from my career in industry, much of the content was written at the time that I was going through the very transition that thousands of others like me have had and will have to make. In the coming pages, we will chart the job hunting journey in three sections. The first section explores the often-overlooked priorities of developing mental safeguards and seeking financial support, as precursors to a successful job hunt. The second section presents a structured approach to the multiple facets of the job application process, from the jobsearch itself right through to receiving a job offer. The final section presents how to navigate the challenges of accepting and rejecting a job offer, and explores the transition to a new role.

If I could turn back time and give myself a single piece of advice, it would be to be open to learning new things as part of continual professional development. This is essential for growing as an individual and in a career perspective. By focusing only on our strengths we miss out on new ideas and experiences, whereas opening ourselves up to change, exposes us to new opportunities. As we go through this book, we'll take note of your strengths but also areas you wish to develop.

Section I:
Laying the foundations

In this section, we'll look at the different factors that affect mental health during the jobsearch, as well as how you can manage them.

Chapter 1:
The mental health impacts of jobseeking

As a young man, I had never thought that I would ever have a mental health issue. I subscribed to the notion that mental ill-health was somehow shameful and should not be admitted. Of course, now I realise how wrong I was. In recent years, awareness of the importance of mental health has increased, and there is starting to be less stigma associated with struggles and illnesses. Looking back, I can see that over the many months of my fruitless jobsearch, my mental health was slowly deteriorating with each passing day. Unlike many physical health issues, the symptoms were not obvious to me, and I was not aware that there are several simple preventative measures everyone can take to protect and nourish their mental wellbeing.

When I searched for information about the link between mental health and unemployment, most of the results I found were focused on unemployment as a consequence of mental health issues. Even now, very few reports seem to present the alternative perspective of how job hunting affects mental health, whether employed or unemployed. My experience, however, was very much the latter – I recognise now that my mental health struggles arose from the decline in both my mental stimulation and physical exercise. And I know I'm not alone with this. The immediate impact of not having a job is, for the vast majority of people, the loss of necessary income. This brings with it financial stress, which can in turn cause jobseekers to reduce their living standards drastically, affecting both their physical and mental health. On the other hand, the employed jobseeker may not have the same financial worries, but they must contend with jobseeking in their limited spare time. They then risk forfeiting a known job for an unknown set of experiences, and both of these pressures bring with them very different strains on mental health.

In academic terms, it is only relatively recently that a link between sudden unemployment and mental health was first realised, as a result of the Great Depression in the 1930s[4]. Similar findings were made after the more recent financial crisis of the late 2000s; this event led to a surge

4   Eisenberg P., Lazarsfeld P.F., (1939) The Psychological Effects of Unemployment, Psychological Bulletin, 35, 358-390

in unemployment and mental health problems[5]. More recently still, the COVID-19 pandemic resulted in job insecurities on a global scale and a decline in physical exercise during the lockdowns. At the time of writing, the full extent of the mental health impact of the pandemic on all of us remains to be seen.

What is clear, however, is that there are numerous factors that contribute to mental health issues. Factors that may impact someone include, among others: financial stress, poor physical health, family pressures, lifestyle, and age. There have been numerous findings that show that as a period of unemployment increases, the mental health problems associated with it deepen. For instance, the National Mental Health Development Unit observed that depression and anxiety can be up to 10 times more prevalent for people who have been unemployed for longer than 12 weeks[6]. Another study found that 18 % of jobseekers who were unemployed for longer than 27 weeks required treatment for depression[7]. A jobseeker's age is an important factor too: a report by The Prince's Trust showed that a quarter of the long-term unemployed aged 16 to 25 had self-harmed, while a third had contemplated suicide[8]. Those over 30 typically face a different set of challenges, such as greater responsibilities to support dependents[9]. So influential is the impact of unemployment specifically – and job hunting more generally – on mental health, that research has even been undertaken to determine how jobseekers' spouses are affected[10]. Clearly, it is fair to say that unemployment is a public health issue.

It took me a while to become fully aware of the effects unemployment was having on my mental wellbeing, as well as the indirect effects such as strains on relationships. With my depression came a gradual but noticeable loss of self-confidence, and I became steadily more irritable and defensive. Although I was

Mental health

There are many ways you can help manage your mental health including noting down how you feel throughout the day in a mood diary. We'll talk about these exercises in the next chapter.

If you are struggling with this at the moment, and want help straight away there are some links at the end of Chapter 2 to some helpful resources. Don't be afraid to reach out for support!

5   assets.publishing.service.gov.uk/government/uploads/system/uploads/attachment_data/file/772596/
    Movement_into_employment_report_v1.2.pdf
6   www.mentalhealth.org.uk/sites/default/files/fundamental-facts-about-mental-health-2016.pdf
7   www.gallup.com/poll/171044/depression-rates-higher-among-long-term-unemployed.aspx
8   www.princes-trust.org.uk/help-for-young-people/news-views/youth-index-2014
9   Clark A.E., Oswald A.J, (1994) Unhappiness and Unemployment, The Economic Journal, 104, 424, 648-659
10 Marcus J., (2013) The effect of unemployment on the mental health of spouses – Evidence from plant closures in Germany, Journal of Health Economics, 32, 3, 546-558

fortunate to not have the financial stresses of paying a mortgage or rent, the absence of income, daily routine, and independence (as a consequence of living at home) brought a bespoke set of insecurities fit to my fears. Even when I became employed, the effects of unemployment lingered for several years, as it took a while for the damage to be undone and for me to recognise what had happened to me. Thankfully, mental illness can be treated with the right support[11] – personally, I gained a lot of help from my network of friends and family – but taking the first step to recognise mental health problems can be difficult. I hope this book helps you identify and prevent the stress, anxiety, and depression that can arise during a jobsearch.

11 Linn M. W., Sandifer R., Stein S., (1985) Effects of Unemployment on Mental and Physical Health, American Journal of Public Health, 75, 5

Chapter 2:
A positive mental attitude

There were three elements of the job hunt process that chipped away at my confidence, and it was only when I recognised them that I was able to address them. The more obvious factor was, of course, the flood of rejected applications I received. Now, much of the jobseeking process is out of your hands, and this is always going to be hard for some people. Of course, some things are in your control: the quality and content of your applications, for example, and how you can structure your day to ensure you are in a healthy state, mentally and physically, to write quality work. Starting from Chapter 4 onwards, this book will focus on how to maximise your job hunting success. The second important factor that affected my mental health was the financial stress of not having any income. If this is something affecting you, we will look at applying for governmental unemployment support in Chapter 3. The final stressor that was limiting my happiness and wellbeing was the loss of any daily routine. Without a job, I did not need to wake up early or leave the house, so I soon lost any structure in my day – the worst thing for my mental state. In this chapter, we'll look at some of the numerous different ways you can add structure to your day, and introduce mental and physical stimulation.

Top activities to improve your mental health

To get through the monotony of endless job applications, I used to daydream about doing some crazy things – like reading the entire dictionary, or walking the full length of the River Thames. These escapist fantasies were neither helpful nor practical, but I eventually realised that there were alternative activities I could do that were just as adventurous but much more worthwhile. For instance, instead of reading the dictionary, I read some cheap novels that I got from a local charity shop. And instead of walking the route of the river, I jogged in the local parks. I turned overly ambitious tasks into more achievable and rewarding activities, which I felt great about when I completed. So, whether it is jobseeking or staying active, the key is to have a series of small achievable targets. Below are activities that can add structure to your day, allow you to develop new skills, and help rebuild your confidence.

Get a notepad

The first thing I would highly recommend is to get yourself a decent notepad. It could be a traditional diary, or a digital tablet; it doesn't matter what you write in, as long as it's easy and pleasant to use. Now you have a special place to write down plans, thoughts and activities, as a way to organise your day, prioritise your tasks, and monitor your progress. The best investment I made during my unemployment was an inexpensive but smart-looking notepad that was suitable for use in an interview. I bookmarked important pages so that I could quickly find them wherever I was, be it looking for jobs at my desk or looking for notes during an interview. I always kept my notebook with me wherever I went, just in case I thought of a great sentence to include in a covering letter.

List your achievements

A great way to develop a sense of accomplishment is to make a list of all the experiences you have encountered and skills you have developed throughout your career, including those part-time roles, voluntary work, or freelance one-off jobs. This will be your vault of achievements that will make you realise you have done more than you think. Better still, when you have written these down, you will have a handy checklist of all the brilliant things you have achieved, which makes for a fantastic confidence booster if you read it just before an interview. We'll look at how to turn those experiences into transferable skills that will bolster your job application and interview, later on in Chapter 5.

Develop a skill

Employers love people with a growth mindset, or those who actively seek to learn and develop new skills, because this enables a company to grow and achieve more. That's why employers invest in training courses for their staff, to allow them to learn new abilities and strengthen existing ones. If you have the opportunity to develop a skill at work, do take it, especially if it complements your existing skillset. If training sessions at work are not available to you, though, there are cheap alternatives you can access at home. For example, if you have no computer modelling experience, there are lots of free YouTube videos of people building models and solving typical Excel problems. If you want to strengthen your language skills, there are lots of free apps like DuoLingo.

Not only are new skills or courses like this a good way to engage your brain and structure your day, they also add to your career experience and boost your confidence. When interviewers asked me about my hobbies, they were impressed when I said that I had taught myself basic Spanish in my spare time. Finding time to develop can be tricky, especially if you are working while looking for another job, but the key is that consistent learning will give you steady progress. So, thirty minutes a day is a better investment of time than two hours once a week. Even today, I devote regular time in my week to learn and develop. For instance, I listen to podcasts on finance while I do the dishes. This helps speed up a boring chore and I can dip in and out whenever I want. Using your list of achievements you can map out where you excel but also which skills you can develop. For example, if you have lots of knowledge in computer science but you need to strengthen your writing skills, you can spend time writing short essays on topics that inspire you. What will you learn?

Unwind & be cathartic

If you want to temporarily escape the tedious, repetitive reality of job hunting, I found indulging in a good book a great way to do so for little to no cost. I visited my local charity shop and found three novels for the price of a coffee, and the easy-to-read fictions were a welcome break to the formal reading and writing that the job application process entails. If reading is not really your jam, I also found that baking was a therapeutic activity to release any built up stress. Icing a cake and kneading soft dough helped my mind to disengage. Plus, at the end of the process I could actually see (and eat) what I had made – which gave me the weekly confidence boost I needed. However you choose to relax, pick something you enjoy and let go of any stresses when you do it.

Get dressed

During the low points of my jobsearch, I began to give up on dressing well. This fuelled a cycle of depression and undermined my confidence. After a while, I realised it broadcast an important message that I had given up. Eventually, I made a conscious effort to conduct my search for employment as if I was working in an office in a regular job. I tried to wake up earlier in the mornings as close to 9:00 am as

Structured days for employed jobseekers

If you are jobseeking while currently employed, it can be very hard to manage your time. The central theme of this chapter is to create a routine that structures the day or week to manage your time better, and although my experience was as an unemployed jobseeker, the same principle holds true for those in employment too. For example, if you are spending 8 hours a day working and an extra hour commuting, breaking down the job application task into smaller more manageable elements can help give you the downtime you need to rest, so you can write a higher quality application.

I could. I took regular breaks, and made sure to change out of my pyjamas! It took a while to overcome the inertia, but the more I began to structure my day, the more my self-esteem began to improve. Simple things like taking regular showers, ironing clothes, wearing a shirt, or getting a haircut helped push me into the mental zone I needed to be. What makes up part of your morning routine – breakfast? A walking 'commute' around the block? Make up? Do you usually read or listen to podcasts on the train, or have a coffee in your car, or do a couple of sun salutations before your morning shower? Whatever works for you, try sticking as close to your daily routine as you can, and don't let yourself fall into the slump of inertia.

Reward yourself

Writing job applications and proofreading your work is tedious and laborious. Having to do this constantly, over a long period of time, requires so much effort and willpower that it can be mentally exhausting unless you have a simple incentive structure. This is standard practice in employment (such as bonuses, employee perks, coffee breaks, etc.), so I thought I'd try to apply it to my jobsearch. I created a simple reward system whereby I set myself specific and achievable targets throughout the week, and rewarded myself when I completed my tasks. These included finishing off a covering letter, proofreading an application, or even improving in a new skill that I was trying to learn.

The rewards were never expensive but they were fun, like visiting a friend, going for a walk, eating a sweet, watching a film or even sipping some wine. What is important though is that the goal is specific (so you know exactly when you have completed it) and achievable, so that you do not doubt yourself. This really helped push me to finish whatever it was I needed to do that week, and it also meant I did not feel guilty for stopping working when I had hit my target.

Socialise

The social element of going to meet friends is great for your mental wellbeing – especially if you find the right way to socialise for your needs and situation. Although dining in a restaurant or partying in a bar can be great fun, they can be expensive ways to spend time with your friends. For example, I found that when I was younger, most of my friends only ever wanted to meet in bars – which was fun, until I recognised that I was drinking more frequently than I wanted to, and I was no longer enjoying it because it was counterproductive to my mental and physical health. It took a lot of energy and effort for me to balance the desire to socialise on terms I was comfortable with, but it was worth it: I created an environment where I was spending less time drinking alcohol, and replacing it with healthier alternatives that were equally sociable, such as walks in the park, or a chat in a coffee shop.

A positive mental attitude

Exercise

Keeping fit is a great way to stay in shape, but also to improve your mental health and develop a daily routine. Jogging, running, or yoga are all great activities that you can do for free in the park. Moreover, being outside raises your vitamin D levels to help prevent depression. You may even be able to find a local activity group that meets regularly so you can exercise as a group; a good way to meet new people. It can be all too easy to stay indoors when you are working from home or unemployed, and a good walk in the fresh air is great for your mental health.

Volunteer

As part of my attempt to create more structure in my day, and a mental transition from thinking I was unemployed to thinking I had work-like activities to do, I looked for nearby volunteering opportunities. I looked for options that allowed me to do something I knew I would be good at, such as public speaking, so that I could enjoy it, but I also looked for something that would teach me a new skill. That way, I could develop myself professionally and improve my employability, while also doing something for other people.

I found a local homeless charity which was looking for someone to teach English and IT skills to their residents once a fortnight. This was perfect for me; it gave me a commitment to make and the weekly structure I was looking for, and provided the mental stimulation and human engagement that had been absent in my day to day life. It also dramatically improved my self-confidence, because I was able to help others and contribute to the community. At the end, I received a certificate that not only gave me a sense of achievement, but also strengthened my job applications. This now meant that I could explain that during the apparent gap in my work history, I continued to develop my communication and leadership skills through my voluntary work.

There are so many benefits to volunteering and so many skills to develop. You get to help others, complete rewarding tasks and you improve yourself. The best thing of all is that there is a wide range of activities to suit all types of people and you can do as little or as much as you like. Here are some example activities that you can find wherever you are:

Preferences	Activity
To be indoors	Edit documents for charities from home
To be outdoors	Litter picking in local parks
To socialise	Go on fun runs for charity

Preferences	Activity
To engage 1-on-1	Visit or phone the elderly
To develop leadership skills	Teach at a homeless shelter

Things to watch out for

As well as the good opportunities to look for, there are some potential mental health pitfalls to avoid. While you are figuring out activities that best help you to build your positive mental attitude, watch out for these mood-busters.

Strains on relationships

We mentioned earlier that the consequences of the stress and exhaustion of job hunting spans beyond your own mental health and can impact your relationship with others. In my experience, acknowledging these strains is a critical first step to resolving them. During my unemployment, my partner at the time was also unemployed but lived on the other side of the country. We only saw each other infrequently because the cost of travel was a barrier. It was also awkward when we did visit each other because we were never alone; I was living at my parents' house and she was sharing a room with friends. The physical distance also placed a lot of emotional strain, and we found that video calls, emails and texts only go so far. This meant that by the time we had both found employment, the psychological stress of distance and unemployment had irreparably strained the relationship. Even relationships with friends and family were affected. If I could go back now, I would love to have told myself that communicating how I felt was essential.

Jealousy

Whenever I socialised with friends it was painful to hear about their career successes and promotions, and difficult to not feel envious. I fixated too much on comparing myself to them and how I had not achieved what they had, which was really unhealthy and began to create some friction. Eventually, I recognised that they were having their own issues that they were dealing with too, and that the grass is not always greener on the other side. I realise now that the target I needed to work towards had to be specific to me, and not what others had achieved. As I have continued through my career, I also realise that a more appropriate measure of my success and development is to compare where I am now and where I was several years ago.

Shotgun applications

The first 30 job applications I submitted were focused on highly technical positions because that is what I thought I was limited to. However, when they were unsuccessful, I began to panic. How on earth would I get a job in any other area if I cannot succeed in the field I specialise in? With self-doubt came depression and I developed an "any job is better than no job" mentality. I began to apply for anything and everything I saw, even if the positions were highly inappropriate for my qualifications. This was a real waste of my time and during one particularly stressful month, I applied for three jobs a day, about 100 in total; almost all were copied and pasted. This exhausted me, but it also added to my depression because all 100 were rejected.

The problem was that almost all were applications to unsuitable positions – but I was not able to see it at the time. Even worse, to the few positions that were actually suitable, the copy and paste approach was easy to detect, not just due to the scattering of spelling errors that lay in them, which is why I wasn't selected for those. What I really needed to do was focus my energy and time making one strong application, rather than firing off bursts of poorly written ones, for unsuitable positions that were poorly paid, and that I would not enjoy even if I was offered them. After I reviewed my approach, and set myself a more realistic target of a strong application or two a week, I began to receive better feedback from the hiring managers, which helped me improve my future applications further. We'll look at how you can better manage your application approach later on in Chapter 4.

Avoid sad music

There is something so soothing about feeling sorry for yourself. I used to wallow melancholically whenever I heard a sad song, but it became unnervingly addictive and only exacerbated my depression. I used to listen to certain songs on repeat so often that I eventually associated them with feeling sad. It got to the stage where if I heard those songs while I was doing something fun my mood would sour instantly, and back into the abyss I would tumble. So, try not to linger in self-pity for too long! I found that a sure bet is to listen to upbeat music to distract you. I know how mentally exhausting it can be to try to remain happy and cheerful, but the alternative, of allowing yourself to sink irretrievably, is far worse.

"I'm definitely getting it"

It is easy to fall into the trap of assuming you will be offered a particular job or that the jobsearch will not be very difficult or time consuming. In my search, I soon realised to my cost that this is simply not the case. At the start of my jobsearch, I only ever applied to one or two jobs at a time because I feared I would not know what to do when I was offered both; looking back, it is laughable how overconfident I was! What I did not know then was that the whole job application process, from the submission right through to the interview and up until the offer is made, can take several months. Even if you are offered a job, it is not guaranteed until you have signed the contract with that employer. So, even if you send off a really strong job application and had a great interview, and you are certain that you will get the position, you should still apply for other jobs. You should not neglect other job opportunities that you come across. There are several reasons for this:

- First, the job that you are 'certain' you will get might still be offered to someone else. And that other job advert you initially neglected might have expired. Then you will feel really bad; this has happened to me too many times.

- Second, you might find that you are fortunate to receive several offers. This provides you with an opportunity to choose which job to accept, and the potential to leverage one in a bid to negotiate a better offer from the other. This is a far better situation to be in than having to accepting the only offer you receive.

- Third, there may be some organisational change within the target company, such as a budget review, that requires the hiring manager to cancel an offer. Even if they promise to re-offer it in a few months when the budget is revised, nothing is ever guaranteed. The company may undergo a merger, or the hiring manger may leave the job, or redundancies mean the job is no longer tenable.

Therefore, making assumptions that you have a guaranteed job based only on an offer without a signed contract is risky. If you can, always apply for other jobs even when you have received a formal offer. It's much easier to turn down an offer than to have to re-start the whole laborious application process. In line with this, if you have a job while you are job hunting, you should never quit your current role until you have a signed a contract with a new employer, for the exact same reasoning. We'll look at how to manage job offers later on in Chapter 9.

                                   A positive mental attitude

Substance abuse

However you decide to spend your recreational time, do take the time to assess whether it is something that is truly what you want to do. You should be aware that some jobs, such as government security positions, require you to disclose your history of alcohol use and drug consumption. If this is something that you need support or guidance on, there are many organisations who provide judgement-free, confidential advice. You can find guidance on mental health and substance abuse by visiting your doctor's surgery or citizen advice bureaus if you prefer face-to-face advice. Don't be afraid to reach out for help!

Chapter 3:
Applying for financial support

In many countries around the world, there is some form of welfare system to support those who are in need. This spans financial, psychological, and educational support, and a range of people may qualify for it, such as carers, expectant parents, the elderly, immigrants, and, of course, jobseekers. In the UK, the Department of Work and Pensions operate an agency called the Jobcentre Plus to provide the support and information people need, and each applicant must formally apply with details of their personal or financial circumstances online. The exact level of financial support you qualify for varies depending on factors such as the number of dependents you have, or the amount of bank savings. Other countries operate a similar system and the mechanics may vary depending on the national and regional legislation.

My story: Seeking financial aid

At the start of my period of unemployment, I decided to move in with my family as I was mostly living on my savings... but as time went on, I eventually ran out of money. It took me a while – and some serious pride-swallowing – but when I finally applied for a jobseeker's allowance, I realised that I was a fool for not doing so earlier.

When I first arrived at the job centre I felt nervous. I had anticipated an environment where endless forms needed to be signed before I received any support, and I was not wrong. I remember my first impression well: four burly, grumpy bouncers blocking the entrance to anyone who hadn't shown their appointment cards. They directed me to the clerk at the furthest desk, where I waited to be seen. From that moment on, and for the next 6 months, that was where I went every fortnight.

The first few times I went, I would always have a skip in my step, as I was glad to get out of the house. Eventually, the fortnightly routine got tiresome and it felt awful when the guards would nod

in acknowledgement as I walked through the door. The sentiment
was friendly but it was also incredibly disheartening.

Part of the reason I was unsuccessful in my jobsearch was
because my employment profile and educational background
meant that a lot of the job adverts and employment resources my
local job centre had to offer were unsuitable. I was over-qualified
and under-experienced, which meant that hardly any jobs coming
through were suitable. Even when I applied to junior or entry-level
positions that offered salaries well below what I was previously
earning, my application would quickly be rejected. After a while, I
realised that my entire job application approach was wrong: from
the language I used in the applications, right through to the roles I
was applying for.

Our friends and family pay taxes for the principal reason to facilitate vital
social welfare to those in need – indeed, if you are in work, or have been, this
is why you pay tax too. However, there is a common negative misconception
that people who claim financial support are somehow trying to cheat the
system and get more than they deserve, and it is for this reason a lot of
people who legitimately qualify for aid do not seek it. I know many people –
including me – who felt guilt or shame at applying for financial relief. It took
a while, but I now realise that there is absolutely no shame in applying for
and receiving income support. That's what it's there for – a safety net to help
those who need it get back on their feet. So, to help you get the most out
of job centres, here are my best tips. This advice is mostly based on the UK
system, but the general principle will apply to most places.

How job centres work

You will likely have to apply online via a government website, which
should be easy to find, unless you have special circumstances and need
to apply in person. Applications are tedious and require a great deal of
personal and financial information, but are a vital first step to register
you on to the centralised government system. Typically, government
departments don't communicate to each other efficiently, nor do offices
within departments. This means that you cannot rely on one clerk finding
your information from a different department readily – so my first tip is
to gather all of your documents, bank statements, payslips or tax forms,
identity documents and so on, before you start.

Once you have registered, you will be assigned to meet with a specific job officer at your nearest job centre for your specific region of the country, with whom you will meet regularly. The aim of each meeting is to provide you with objective feedback on how you have been searching for jobs, and advise improvements to your approach. These meetings also allow you to ask for further assistance such as computer training or applying for loans. A consequence of working within a government office is that government policy is applied strictly, which often means that job officers have to make decisions in line with these guidelines. As a result, they have a reputation for appearing unsympathetic. For example, tardiness is unacceptable and can result in tough sanctions, such as withholding all of the aid you are due. This has been a source of mistrust between the applicants and the officers – but remember, they are only trying to do their job. As frustrating as the system can be, I recommend doing your best to work with it – so make sure you leave plenty of time to get to your appointments.

Additional financial support can include discounted travel on public services as well as reimbursement of reasonable travel expenses. You may be entitled to continued support right up to starting a new role, which is designed to fill in any financial gaps between jobseeking and full employment. In some cases, you may be allowed to claim financial aid in addition to earning income via a part time job, but this is determined on a case by case basis.

At the job centre

Check the noticeboards: Job adverts and updates are usually posted on noticeboards in the job centres as well as online. Check both regularly and sign up for updates. The information that is posted also includes training sessions you may be eligible for. I once saw an advert for free Uber rides to interviews! Another advert I saw was for a nearby recruitment drive, so it really can be worth your while.

Check updates: Changes in government policy can occur that affect how a job centre operates, its working hours, and even the aid you receive.

Ask for training sessions: There are lots of coaching sessions to improve your CV and IT skills, as well as self-help sessions for drug & alcohol abuse. However, you might have to ask for these and there may be a restriction on how many you can attend, so make sure to pick the ones that you think you will find most helpful.

Save money sensibly

The financial situation of one jobseeker might be very different from another. I was fortunate enough to live with my parents and didn't need to pay rent. However, although the financial stress was limited, it was not eliminated. There was also the added emotional stress, such as a loss of independence, that living with parents can bring. Whatever your situation is, below are sensible suggestions to help your money go a little further.

Budgeting

This might sound obvious, but there is a knack to saving money sensibly. It is horrible to have to count your pennies constantly to see if you can afford something, whether it is a bus ticket or a sweater, but you don't have to be miserly. I made a list of my weekly expenditures, and ranked them in order of importance. I then made a budget and realised I could save at least £20 a month by replacing expensive snacks and junk food with healthier alternatives. By the end of the month I had enough to spend on a treat like seeing a film or eating at a restaurant. I was even able to buy some much needed new shoes for £50 because I had saved sensibly.

Innovative companies like Monzo and Revolut allow you to visually track and limit your spending automatically. They also have a 'round up' feature whereby you they round up the price on purchases you make, and save the difference in a savings account. Some really like this automatic feature, while others don't. Whichever method you prefer, monitoring your spending can help you work towards reducing it incrementally.

Manage debt

I recently came across a book called Real Life Money by Clare Seal, who documents her struggle to reduce her debt of over £25000. One of the key messages I learnt was to manage debt as a priority during periods of job insecurity. An example, which I had not considered, is to ask your bank for a reduced interest rate or fees on any outstanding loan payments. This approach might not always work with a bank, but it does not hurt to ask.

Socialising

Buying drinks for your friends in a 'round' at the bar is ingrained into British society, so it was really difficult for me to stop doing this when I socialised, despite living on a tight budget. On reflection, it seems so ridiculous – but there is an extraordinary unspoken pressure to buy each other rounds. Nowhere else in the world seems to have this quirky feature and it can leave you out of pocket. However, I eventually stopped buying drinks when I realised that I was spending so much money on alcohol. I simply declined drink offers so I did not feel obliged to buy rounds, and only bought what I consumed. The truth is, supportive friends will understand.

In for a penny

Fewer and fewer of us are using cash and around 50% of all transactions are by card. However, like most people, I had a few coins stashed away on old clothes, winter coats, and in the kitchen drawers. So, I started a makeshift piggy bank and saved all the loose change I found around the house. Eventually I counted them out and put them in my bank account. I found a whopping £78, so you might want to start looking down the back of your sofas...

Discounts

Loyalty cards are a great way to receive discounts on everyday purchases like coffee, food, or shopping. There are also lots of online cashback sites that reward you when you buy from preferred customers. For example, Quidco pay you a small percentage of the cost of your purchase if you buy via their website.

Thrift stores

You can save lots of money by buying clothes like jumpers or jackets from charity shops. Not only does this support the charities, it avoids the premium you pay for new clothes in high-street shops. This definitely applies to books too! You could save some money by using free online websites like Free-cycle to get used stuff that other people want to throw away. I know people who have exchanged things like tables, chairs, sofas and even TVs in this way. You can also make some money by selling unwanted items in your garage, bedroom, cupboard and even kitchen!

Transport

If you need to get around, look for discount travel deals for bus, rail or coach services. Car-share apps like Uber are also options to consider but can be less reliable and more expensive. There are also several cashback sites that can offer you discounts on journeys booked via their website, so keep an eye out for that. Some routes, like long distance train rides, might be cheaper if you buy tickets that split the route into its constituent parts. For instance, if you wish to travel from A to B, several tickets for stops in between the two might be cheaper than the direct ticket. Alternatively, you might try walking if where you're going is close by. Not only will this save you some money, but it's a great way to incorporate exercise into your day.

Section 2:
The application process

In this section, we'll look at how to develop a structured approach to your job hunt, including how to maximise search results, highlight your strengths, and connect with the hiring managers.

Chapter 4:
Searching for jobs effectively

The jobsearch is made up of two interlinked parts: knowing *where* to look for job adverts; but also *how* to look for them. While the former is important for helping you find jobs, it's the latter which helps you identify ones that are best suited to you and your needs. Before you even get to how or where, though, you need to be ready to look: we'll go through this first.

Marketing yourself

You may have heard that you have to "sell yourself" to an employer. I had too, but I never realised how apt this phrase was until recently. In so many ways, a job search is a potential transaction between you and your 'customer' or employer. The product or service you are offering is you, and your ability to fulfil their needs. Of course, you would expect fair payment for this, with the specific remuneration or working conditions reflective of the market. Similarly, an employer needs specific services to function, and would expect to buy them at a rate that is both reflective of the market but also on how well suited that product is to its needs. I'll talk more about this in Chapter 9 on negotiations, but the key message is that companies will only hire what they specifically need, and understanding what they are looking for gives you information that allows you to better market what you can offer. Specifically, you are better equipped to highlight particular skills to suit different companies and job positions. So, before you start looking for jobs to sell yourself to, and before you can sell yourself on paper in a job application, you need to know how to market (or present) yourself with a clear, concise job profile. This is where I initially struggled, because I had not developed a clear message of who I was, what I could do, and what I wanted.

Hiring managers and recruiters actively find candidates through online searches for specific search terms, such as 'data analysis' or 'energy research', but they will filter the candidates based on what they perceive to be suitable. This is why curating your profile to give a clear message is important, to both attract the correct audience and help you stand out from the thousands of other applicants. You may have a range of experiences that contribute to an overall skillset that is unique to you. Highlighting that unique skillset is what will help you to stand out and sell your abilities. Here are some brief examples of the type of skills you can leverage based on different experiences:

Experience	Key transferable skills
Editing	High quality written communication
Lab technician	Attention to detail
Web developer	Active client management
Freelance Tutor	Public speaking
Desk based research	Project ownership

Some experiences will yield more than one skill, and you have the flexibility to highlight one over the other, to suit different applications, as part of curating your profile. Once you've found the key qualities you need to highlight, you can use them to promote yourself when searching for jobs online and when you have direct conversations with colleagues or hiring managers – and you'll be ready to seek out the right jobs in the right places, those which are most likely to buy what you're marketing.

Search effectively

When I first started applying for jobs, I thought that you should only apply for one role at a time, because I was unaware how the job market worked. I was also afraid of the awkwardness of handling two simultaneous interviews if I was successful. I now realise how naïve and impractical this attitude is, and that the reality of the competitive nature of the job market (even before a recession) means that to keep a one-at-a-time approach is much less effective. Multiple concurrent applications ensure you maximise your chances of success and that you do not miss out on great opportunities. However, this can be exhausting if you don't have a structured approach.

Specific search terms

The world is full of job adverts, and phrases such as 'data' or 'research' are increasingly used for non-academic roles. To help you find a suitable job advert, use search qualifiers to specify what you are or are not looking for. For example, you can search for one word or phrase along with a second word or phrase by including the search term "OR":

"Best ways to prepare for a job interview" OR "How to prepare for a job interview"

The above search logic will search for both phrases, which can help narrow down your search to help you find exactly what you're looking for. Another technique I employ is using the plus sign "+" between two words, to force results with an exact match of the terms. For example "Policy + Research Jobs" will help you distinguish between different types of research positions.

Managing your findings

Occasionally, there can be a drought of job adverts for a few days, and then suddenly a great explosion of opportunities the week later, which makes managing the jobsearch process difficult. Finding a suitable job advert is great, but it is important to balance the time you spend on searching with the time you spend on applying for the job opportunities you've found. Something that I found helped me structure my approach was to schedule time for jobsearching and applying. Whenever I found a job advert I liked the look of, I bookmarked it to review it later, rather than immediately apply for it. After I had amassed a few relevant adverts, I spent the next few days examining them in more detail, ranking them, filtering them on suitability, and then applying for the most relevant only. This technique suited my working style as I can be easily distracted, so by forcing myself to only focus on searching, or applying, I enhanced my productivity. You may find you prefer searching for jobs each morning, and writing applications in the afternoon. Or you might prefer to spend two days searching, and the rest of the week writing. Try out different styles to see which works best, but I found that it's best to have a mixture of activities (searching, writing, proof reading etc.) to break up the monotony and create a structured approach.

Managing multiple applications

You are better off investing your time and energy in applying for a job you prefer than one you don't, because you will be more motivated and write a better application. Additionally, an application with an earlier deadline is a higher priority than one that has only just appeared. But how you determine which jobs to apply for when they overlap in deadline, or suitability, is entirely personal. If I had two deadlines close together, I prioritised the job I was most interested in.

I kept a record of the best job adverts I found, their deadlines, and the progress of the application. This helped me re-evaluate the priority of subsequent job applications. For example, I once had two applications to submit by the end of the day but I became ill. I knew it would be a struggle to complete both applications well, so I focused on the one I was more likely to get. One good application is better than two poorly written ones!

Save job adverts

Job adverts do not stay online indefinitely, and if you've applied for multiple jobs with similar sounding roles, at different companies, it can be difficult to remember what the advert specified and what you wrote in your application. This is especially true if you are contacted many weeks after your application. For this reason, I always save a copy of both the job advert and my application in a suitably named folder.

Essential Vs desirable

A typical job advert may have a list of essential skills that employees need, to perform the basic functions of a role, while any additional skills may only be considered desirable. Once recruitment teams receive applications, they review each to score how they meet the job requirements. Over the years I have learnt from contacts in HR that this is a very idealised list, and often companies will interview candidates even if they do not meet all the criteria, depending on the circumstances. For example, if it is essential you have an accounting qualification for a finance position, there won't be much flexibility there. However, if that qualification is only desirable, and you meet most of the other criteria, the recruiter may be open to hiring you, as you can learn any missing competencies as part of the role. A consequence will be that you may have less negotiating power in the interview though. Now consider that you don't quite meet all the required criteria, but you have excellent background knowledge or some other useful skill that you feel makes you a strong candidate, such as confident communication. The best thing you can do is call the assigned contact for queries, such as the recruiter or the hiring manager, to find out if they would be open to your application. If they say yes and advise you to apply, you now stand a better chance because you will be a stand out candidate with a reputation of being proactive. We'll cover how essential and desirable criteria are measured during an interview in Chapter 7.

Using the right language

Each industry has its own jargon, which can be confusing if you are transitioning to a new sector. Using the correct language in your jobsearch will help you attract the right recruiter and avoid unsuitable positions. For example, an executive position might sound senior but it can often mean a junior worker. Below are some examples which may vary depending on the industry or company.

Business terms	Common meaning
Stakeholder, Partner	Client, or collaborator
Service provider, Delivery partner	Supplier

Business terms	Common meaning
Deliverables, Solutions	Output
Decision maker, C-suite	Company director
Consultant, Specialist	Technical lead
Associate	Junior (a step below the next rank)
Associate director, Vice president	Senior Manager

Bad adverts

A company may pay several jobsites to advertise an open position to maximise the pool of candidates it might reach and to manage the recruitment process. In most cases when you click apply, you will be led to the company's main application portal, and the companies track the number of applications to determine if they spent their money wisely. However, it is increasingly common for jobsites to host job adverts that direct you to another job site, rather than the original company. Not only is this counterintuitive for two rival jobsites to collaborate, it is painfully frustrating and time consuming as you hop between the different job sites. This is especially annoying if each new site requires you to create a new profile to view the job advert. Sadly, these 'copy-cat' job adverts may remain online for weeks after the original job vacancy expires. I find the best way to by-pass this is to copy a specific section of the job advert and search for that text instead. You will find all the jobsites hosting this, and one of them will lead you directly to the correct application portal, or recruiter.

Some job adverts intentionally limit specific information about the role, such as job location and salary. This is to encourage you to contact the recruiters directly. On other occasions, the information is incorrect, or poorly edited, which may be a sign that the advert has been copied poorly. This might indicate that the recruiter may not be managing that advert well or fully understand the role's requirements, especially if there is a technical component. You may find reaching out to the recruiter to be a good first step to clarify anything you are unsure of. If you get a bad feeling about a job advert, my experience is to trust your instincts.

Contact the hiring manager

Directly contacting the company you wish to work for is a great way to learn more about a specific role. For example, I applied for a technical sales manager at a high-tech instrument manufacturer, and never heard back for over a month. On the company's job portal the application status had remained as 'pending' so I decided to call the HR department to see if there was an update. I eventually got through to the internal recruiter who told me they were waiting for a candidate to respond to an offer. When that candidate eventually declined, I was consequently invited for an interview. Sadly, I was unsuccessful in the interview for that particular role, but my proactive approach and job experience, had really impressed the HR manager so she was happy to consider me for a more suitable role. This approach might not always work, or it might not be easy to get through to HR, but if you do not try, you may never know.

This kind of proactivity is highly valued in industry, especially in sales driven environments or ambitious businesses focused on rapid growth. Of course, you may be turned away, or redirected to a more suitable person when you call up, in which case you have lost nothing, but you will have left a positive impression. You may even be considering for alternative positions in the future. This approach is very different from the slower pace of academia where emails rather than phone calls are the norm. Bear in mind that it is best to approach the contact provided in a job advert. There will be positions or sections of industry where directly contacting the hiring manager is discouraged. This could be due to the nature of their position or industry, such as a hospital director, or it could be that the hiring manager is not prepared for, or expecting, contact outside of the hiring process. In this case, a phone call from a stranger could be seen as an intrusion rather than a good use of initiative. In such instances, though, a point of contact such as a recruiter will be assigned to answer any questions, so you should definitely talk to them. The aim is to appear proactive, keen, and aware of the company's needs – not attention-grabbing or self-involved!

Some companies wait until the application deadline has passed before reviewing the applications, but there are a few organisations that stipulate they may hire a suitable candidate before the deadline. For this reason, reaching out to the recruitment team early will help you gauge if the opportunity is worth pursuing, all while raising your profile with the company.

Where to find jobs

Now that we've covered how to market yourself and search for jobs effectively, you're ready to go out and look for opportunities that suit you. The traditional approach is to search for job adverts when they appear, but a more proactive approach is to use your network of friends and colleagues to help you identify live opportunities and future openings that are in development. Consider which approach works best for you.

Networking

Professional networking sites, such as LinkedIn, allow you to engage with your existing contacts and meet prospective hiring managers or employees. By far, LinkedIn is the most widely used professional networking site with more than 400 million members in over 200 countries, but it is dominated by experienced industry profiles. This can make it intimidating for less experienced postgraduates who may start with a modest profile. However, the more people you connect with, the wider your network will be, and the more exposed you become to opportunities. And be open-minded: opportunities can include job adverts, but also interesting articles that you can use to initiate conversations with new contacts, which will help expand your network. You can quickly make a name for yourself in various online communities by commenting, sharing or interacting with anyone, from any business, regardless of their seniority. These contacts may help facilitate introductions to companies, further opportunities, or hiring managers you need to speak with. I've made long-term contacts with senior managers and sold to company directors just by engaging with them, and posting articles on industry hot-topics. However, you do need to be patient as this entire process takes time and should be a part of building your online 'brand' or, in other words, marketing yourself – just as we explored at the beginning of this chapter.

It is very daunting starting a new social profile with only a handful of contacts, such as your friends. But, your network extends beyond friends, and includes previous work acquaintances, lecturers, or whomever you have had a good relationship with, especially if connection to them demonstrates your professional skills in some way. This is a valuable resource of knowledge, skills, and experiences, which you can often tap into to get important information. You can ask about hiring opportunities in a specific company, or you can ask how well a general sector is doing following new legislation or a recession, as these may affect hiring budgets.

For example, prior to accepting a job offer where I currently work, I reviewed the profiles of typical current employees to gauge what skills or experiences the company tended to hire. I then approached one person who had recently started there and I simply asked him for a few minutes of his time, to discuss his thoughts on the company and answer some specific questions. He accepted and over the course of 30 minutes I realised how excited he was about the company and it really swayed me. Now, he is a close contact and in exchange, I am proactive to give him information to return the favour.

Another example is actually where one of my contacts reached out to me.

He was a senior manager who I had once asked for assistance. Now, he wanted to cash in that favour, and asked me to let him know of any senior leadership positions in the innovation sector I identified. I could have easily said no, but that would have undermined the symbiotic relationship that grows a network. I was happy to repay the favour because it was such a simple task, but by assisting him, I strengthened that relationship, so in future there is a connection I can count on should I be in need of some minor assistance. This is all networking means – it's a two-way relationship that you build with people.

Asking your network for minor assistance, such as reviewing your presentation, is a great way to get objective feedback you can use to strengthen your application. I felt embarrassed to ask friends for help at first, but in reality most of my friends were usually willing to help, provided I asked for something specific and reasonable. For example, I asked a colleague in Finland if he knew of any temporary work opportunities I could apply to. I used to regularly proofread his work, so he knew I was good at copy-editing, so he suggested I apply for a freelance editing role. I would never have thought of this had I not contacted him. I applied for the opportunity he suggested and got accepted. This soon provided a steady source of temporary income and work structure to my day. It also allowed me to strengthen my CV. Now, instead of a gap in my work history, I had freelance work experience in communication, which is a strength I particularly wanted to highlight.

Jobsites

Networking is crucial, but don't rely on other people to spot job opportunities for you. Jobsites, such as Indeed and Monster, are great for finding broad job roles across diverse sectors, but they tend to be less relevant for highly specialised technical roles. For those, specialist sites like ResearchGate or NewScientist are available which promote technical, academic, and commercial roles in science. There are other industry sites, too, so there may well be one for your particular niche. Whichever jobsite you use, all allow the candidates to describe their work history and previous job duties, but the target audiences will be different. So you will need to tailor your profile and description of work experiences to suit the specific language and requirements of that reader. This is why it is so important to know how to market yourself. Be aware that jobsites do have several shortcomings including the fact that creating online profiles are tedious and that they often host expired adverts. Even worse, some adverts direct you to an endless chain of other jobsites which can be such an infuriating waste of time. See earlier in the chapter on how to search for job adverts effectively and avoid bad ones.

Job fairs

Both virtual and physical job fairs present a further alternative opportunity to meet potential employers face-to-face. You can also have your job profile checked by HR companies, attend small employment workshops, and grow your network. The world's biggest employers may also have their own recruitment drives, while certain industries may host their own industry specific events. It can be a bit daunting approaching employers or other attendees, but after a while, you realise that everyone at such events is actively looking for something, so striking up a conversation to find out what that is can help you quickly determine if there is an opportunity for you or not. Always be prepared to introduce yourself concisely as this will help the audience determine if you are the opportunity they are looking for. I met a fresh graduate at a renewable energy exhibition in Rotterdam who was actively speaking to managers in green technology companies because that is the field he was passionate about joining. People are really receptive to this proactive approach and on his business card was a link to his CV, contact details and a brief introduction to who he was, what he could do, and what he wanted. This was a great approach!

Recruitment services

Networking is great if you are active online, but if you find it difficult to approach people or if you need assistance finding the right job for you, consider working with a recruiter. These are employment professionals who help companies find employees, and help employees find work. Within the recruitment industry is a spectrum of services and activities, for all types of industry. Typically, recruiters receive a brief from a client, who is looking for a list of candidates with a specific set of desirable skills, for a specific role. At one extremity are the more well-known recruitment agencies which operate within their area of speciality, such as office staffing. They will offer a wide range of staff solutions (office managers, telesales callers etc.) to a similarly broad client base, such as department stores, call centres, and restaurants. However, the abundance in competition means profit margins are low as agencies seek to be more competitive. This means their business model is to process a high turnover of jobseekers to satisfy the demand of their numerous clients. These agencies will quickly find you work, but the drawback is that the choice of position is limited. Signing up with an agency will typically involve a short interview and possibly a competency test, such as computer literacy, depending on the agent.

At the other end of the spectrum are executive search firms (head hunters), which operate in an almost opposite way. Executive search companies are typically small, but comprise a team of highly qualified

                    Searching for jobs effectively

graduates and employees with many years of industry experience. They seek exclusive agreements with their clients to fill business critical positions, such as chief executives, heads of department, or other senior positions. The candidates may be passive jobseekers rather than active job hunters, so there is much more focus on engaging with the candidate to lure them to a new role. These are ideal if you are looking for a very specific, high-profile role that requires a bespoke touch.

In between the two extremities are specialised recruitment agencies which focus on niche markets, such as technical sales or science writing. The approach these agents use is a blend of the above, usually involving graduates with limited industry knowledge who search for viable candidates, both active and passive, to satisfy numerous roles. These are ideal agents if you are looking for an entry-level or middle-management position in a new industry. The main difference between the different recruitment companies is the level of candidate engagement and the industry knowledge, but they ultimately function in the same way. They receive a commission from the client so they really want to help you find a job because that is how they get paid. However, this can mean their interests may not always align with yours, such as encouraging you to apply for a position you do not want.

Recruiters may have a more established relationship with the target company you're interested in, so they are perfect for getting your foot in the door. Moreover, they will usually be working on different roles, which means that they can potentially put you forward for different opportunities. This is a great way to maximise your chances of getting an interview. They may even advise you on how to edit your written application which is a great way to get an objective review of your work. Recruiters also play a role in managing both candidates' and clients' expectations - making sure that all parties have a realistic understanding of the job market. However, recruiters are essentially working for you almost for free (until they get paid by the client at the end) so they need you to show commitment and to demonstrate you are worth their time. Here's how to get the most out of working with a recruitment agent:

- Recruiters conduct online searches for profiles that match key words for a specific role they are looking to fill, such as "Prince2" or "sales experience." To be on their radar, tailor your profile to suit a specific job role.

- If they've sent you a job description prior to a call with you, prepare a set of key experiences you can describe that demonstrates how you meet the job requirements. That way, recruiters can quickly identify how best to promote you to their client. The easier you make their lives, the more they will want to work with you.

- Some recruiters place their company's logo in the header of your application so ask to see a copy before it goes out, to check the overall design or layout of the page looks presentable.

- You should receive an alert if they have put your application forward. Keep these saved as they have the contact reference numbers you need to follow up a specific role, such as asking for feedback.

- You might find it helpful to work with several recruiters. However, if two competing recruiters want to put you forward for the same role, it is considered best practise to decide which of the two you want to put you forward. Otherwise, you risk harming your reputation with the hiring manager and the recruiters because they will find out.

- When you accept a job offer, do let recruiters know you are no longer seeking their services. This is a good way to maintain a positive working relationship as you may wish to work with them in future. You want them to think of you when a new opportunity becomes available that matches what you want.

Chapter 5: Writing applications

When you have found a suitable role to apply for, you will need to submit supporting information to verify how you meet the required experience. This is typically in the form of a summary of your recent or most relevant employment history, qualifications, and education. The specific content and detail of the summary can vary significantly. For example, academic positions may want a detailed list of publications, while artistic roles will require a portfolio of your artwork. Similarly, for commercial or managerial roles you will need to demonstrate competence in sales or leadership, respectively. In most parts of the world, especially in European countries, the employment summary is the CV while other parts of the world, such as USA and Canada, it is called a résumé. Whatever you call it, it should contain the same fundamental information on employment background, skills, and accomplishments. In some countries, you may be required to include personal details, such as citizenship status, or ID number. If you're unsure whether to include this information, always reach out to the point of contact for the role.

Tailoring your application

When competition is fierce and there is a high influx of applicants, hiring managers look for applications that stand out. Tailoring your application to match what the employer is searching for will help you do this. Employers look for two kinds of competencies: Hard skills, which include technical knowledge you need to fulfil a role, such as familiarity with legislation; and soft skills, or transferable skills, which are linked to your personality, such as your confidence in communication.

When I first started applying for commercial jobs in industry, I only used a single CV that focused on my technical and academic knowledge. It took me a long time to realise this approach was not highlighting the most relevant skills or experiences, and I was underselling myself. What I should have done was explain how my technical knowledge and experiences gave me the required transferable skills and competencies. By doing so, I would have communicated my capabilities in a language that industry used, rather than the one academia uses. I needed to speak the language of my target, not my starting point.

For example, I used to think that my key strengths, as a former researcher in solar-cell materials, were limited to researching complicated material properties and explaining them concisely to an audience. For this reason I only applied to technical roles, at first, because that is all I thought I could do. However, I eventually realised I was focusing too much on the technical aspect of my experiences, rather than realising the transferable element. Instead, I could have argued that my ability to digest complicated, technical, information and convey it succinctly makes me a suitable candidate as a recruitment consultant, a salesperson, or a journalist. Of course, these different occupations require that communication strength to be described in specific ways, tailored to their unique requirements. When I tailored my applications, I soon noticed I received more positive feedback, which gave me more confidence in future applications.

Your suitability for a role will depend on how much of each type of hard or soft skill you possess. Most hard skills are not immediately transferable, but may provide you with experience that is. For example, the ability to build a robotic prototype is a hard skill. However, if you overcame repeated mechanical challenges in the prototype construction, your experience may include resilience to failure, or problem solving skills. Similarly, if you had to buy expensive, specialist equipment to fix the prototype, which required you to negotiate with the suppliers, you could talk about how resourceful you are. Below are a few examples of hard and soft skills you can use to help tailor your job applications.

Hard skill	Transferable soft skill
Familiarity with government legislation	Comprehension of complicated information
Developing models in Excel	Critical attention to detail
Calculating chemical concentrations	Numerical literacy
Handling customer complaints	Comfortable under pressure
Lecturing on particle physics	Confident public speaking

Some skills or experiences might not be relevant to all the jobs you're applying for. So, favour those which highlight how you fulfil the needs of the role, and archive those that don't. You never know when an experience might be useful to mention in a future interview.

CV layout

Below is a template I use for my CV when applying for industry positions. I never go over two sides of A4, and to maximise readability, I add as much space between the paragraphs as I can, because no one wants to read through large blocks of text. Being able to concisely describe what you achieved is a highly valued skill. Academic CVs will differ to industrial ones in both size and content: for example, it is the norm in most academic fields to include a list of publications, which may require you to go over two pages, but this will be much less relevant in an industry CV. Exciting graphics or fancy margins may look nice, but they are more time consuming than they are valuable, unless you are applying for positions where graphic design is helpful.

Personal details

I have my name, phone, and email details at the top, but I avoid including anything too personal such as my full address, a photo or my age, as these are unnecessary. I also include a short hyperlink to my LinkedIn page rather than typed out as I think this looks visually unattractive. Any recruiter printing off your CV will have a digital copy so can check your profile easily, without having to search too hard.

Profile

Next, I have a short profile section that summarises the entire application in no more than three sentences. This is literally the first impression you give, so make it punchy and concise. I find the following approach helps me introduce myself succinctly:

1. **Who I am:** e.g. Motivated, commercially-minded individual with a background in the energy sector

2. **What I do:** e.g. Confident public speaker with a strong ability to communicate to diverse audiences

3. **What I want:** e.g. Passionate about developing a career with a science-focused business

Key skills

If you are lacking in experience, you may wish to add a small line to briefly highlight the top three or four skills you have. As you gain experience this section might become redundant, and removing it can free up some space on the CV.

Experience

This is where you detail how your experience meets the job requirements. You can generally be quite flexible in how you present this, but try to describe your roles chronologically, with your most recent role first. If your job role has an unusual name that is not common to all industries, you should consider briefly explaining the key function. You can always justify this in the interview.

Hiring managers will understand that companies change names, or that you may have worked at the same company several times with gaps in between. What really matters is that you provide sufficient detail of your job function and any metrics of achievement.

Education

Here you can list your most relevant education and qualifications. This does not need to be exhaustive but you should add details such as the university or vocational topic you studied, and grade achieved.

Achievements

This is a great place to demonstrate extracurricular activities or achievements that might give you an edge over competitors. For example, competency in first aid or language skills, or any awards you've won. Some details such as a valid driving licence may not be suitable unless the roles states you will need to travel.

Hobbies

There are arguments for and against including this section. Highlighting your extracurricular activities is a great way to round off an application and show your personality but only if it is a short, concise sentence. Conversely, it might not always be suitable to include it for all job applications, and as I now seek to apply to more managerial level roles, I no longer include it. This allows me to free up more space on the page so that I can add extra detail elsewhere.

Metrics of success and performance

It is easy to list out a set of generic duties you performed in your past work experience, but a stronger application describes in sufficient detail what you achieved in your various roles. Think of these questions as a guide when you describe your role:

- What did you do and what was the reason?

- Can you list or quantify a specific achievement?

- Can you indicate the outcome of that work?

- Have you ever exceeded the expectations of your role?

Examples	Questions
Worked as a junior buyer, saving the company money by negotiating a better deal from a supplier	How much money did you save them? What was your function in the negotiation?
Leading a team to solve problems	What kind of problems did you solve? What was the outcome?
Working on new product launches	How successful was the launch? Did it result in increased sales or a product award?
Generating sales and business in a critical market	How much did you sell? Which market did you sell to?

These questions will be running through the minds of recruiters so they can gauge your performance. You can add value to your job application by adding that extra detail, without increasing your word count massively. Below are examples of questions you might want to answer to quantify your achievement.

Covering letter

I use a simple but effective template when I write a covering letter, which I break up into three sections and keep strictly to one side of A4. First, I have a brief introduction of my profile; I want to quickly introduce who I am, what I do and why I want the role. I then explain how relevant my experience is to the skills I have identified as critical for the role. If you are lacking some of the skills, focus on what you do have, and demonstrate how these existing experiences, in combination with an ambition to develop new skills, makes you suitable for the role. I always finish with a snappy summary of how my key skills make me a highly suitable candidate for the role.

Different application styles

Many organisations employ their own format for job applications, which can differ across industry. For example, you may be required to complete multiple choice questionnaires, or you may be restricted to viewing the webpages in order. It is important to identify what an application fully requires before you prepare your submission, so you can plan your time and schedule accordingly.

Universities

Most universities have their own, unique application system, typically due to archaic or legacy websites that are too expensive to update. This might include completing a downloadable document that is protected from formatting, which can be very frustrating to write in. Others may require the applicant to write paragraphs online about how they meet specific competency criteria, without the need to attach any paperwork.

Large organisations

Companies that hire applicants in large numbers tend to have their own sophisticated application systems. These typically involve answering targeted questions to quantify your competence. Usually, you are unable to contact the HR team directly, but all the information you need will be online and there are often lots of helpful videos and detailed instructions to guide your applications.

Submitting an application

Below are a selection of handy tips to add structure to your application process.

Save your submissions: Saving a copy of your completed application will help you quickly identify what you submitted, should you be invited for an interview several months later.

Save the job advert: This is useful if you've applied for similar roles at several companies, as job adverts disappear without warning.

Proofread your application: Teaming up with a friend to review each other's work is a great way to quickly spot mistakes as you often miss them on your own.

Update your CV: Save a master copy of your CV to record your skills and update it every 6 months as you develop new experiences.

Keep it simple: Your application should be concise and easy to read. Help the reader by avoid adding unnecessary words and unexplained acronyms.

Job site applications

Some job sites allow you to apply for jobs with a single click, which simply sends your profile to the hiring manager without the need to laboriously re-write a bespoke application or covering letter. However, do remember to ensure you have the most up to date and accurate details on your profile.

Transferring between roles

You may be interested in moving to another team within the same company, or a different department, perhaps. Occasionally, you may come across secondment opportunities: these are intended to facilitate a temporary knowledge transfer to a complementary company, such as a subsidiary of your main employer. I was in such a situation, and I found that it can be very tricky to indicate your interest without raising suspicion with your existing team. In my experience, the best thing to do is find out as much information about the role as you can before you formally apply. If your company is big enough, there may be an intranet advertising these opportunities, or you may see them advertised online. You may even like

My story: Applying for a secondment

I was working for a very temperamental, inexperienced and insecure manager, who made my life miserable. So, when the opportunity to transfer to another team came, I jumped at it. I met with the hiring manager to learn about the role. I thought I was playing it cool by not explicitly saying I was interested in applying, because I was nervous that my manager would find out, but on reflection it was pretty obvious what I was doing. I used the meeting to talk through my job experience and skills, highlighting relevant achievements. Sadly, though, the budget for the new role fell through and it was no longer a viable opportunity. I had asked the hiring manager for discretion but eventually my manager found out. I was under no obligation to tell him, but he was upset that I hadn't. When he asked why I did not ask his permission, I casually told him the truth, that all I did was ask for further information.

It's normal to be concerned about what your own manager might say about your aspirations, but the truth is that there is nothing wrong with having a conversation. Some companies require you to inform your manager before you formally apply to work with another department, so look for policy documents at your company if you are unsure.

to approach an existing employee in the team that is hiring, to find out what it is like to work there. This way you will have an initial idea of the role and the working conditions before you've even alerted anyone to your intentions. The next step is to arrange a private informal chat with the hiring manager, but be aware they will use this as an opportunity to interview you and determine your suitability. This is why it is essential to present your capabilities clearly and prepare beforehand.

If you are applying for a position within the company that you currently work for, you may happen to know the interviewer or hiring team personally. However, in many parts of the world companies must advertise job vacancies publicly so you may come up against external candidates. It is easy to be lulled into a false sense of security when you know your interviewers. Try to approach the entire application process with the same focus you would for an external job advert. This means developing a strong argument on how you have the right skills for the job, even though it may seem obvious.

How to handle an unsuccessful application

Receiving an outcome to an application can take as little as a few days, but may take several weeks or even months in some cases; the time it takes will depend on many factors outside of your control, such as the number of applicants, budget constraints, business priorities, availability of the hiring manager etc. It is incredibly frustrating to learn your application has been unsuccessful, but it's even worse when you do not hear the results of your application for weeks on end or even at all. Most employers give applicants a guide on the timeframe within which they will respond, and if you've not heard back within that time, you are left to assume you have not been successful. Please do be prepared for the silent treatment – whether it's right or not, it is the reality of the situation. Here's a statistic for you: only 20% of my applications were ever formally recognised as unsuccessful – the rest were simply ignored. This is obviously very frustrating, but it is a sad truth that many companies just do not have the time or capacity to reply to every candidate, especially if the process is not automated.

If you do receive an answer that your application was unsuccessful, you should definitely reply asking for feedback. You may not get it, especially prior to the interview stage, but it's a great habit to form. Not only does it make you look good, by demonstrating that you are a mature candidate who is keen to improve, but more importantly, you may get information which will help improve your future applications. I always chased for feedback and most of the time I never heard back, but there have been several memorable moments where I did – and on two occasions I even booked an interview as a consequence. This is because recruiters, and employers, love proactive candidates.

If I could go back in time, I would tell myself that it is so valuable to take time to reflect on what went well, what went wrong, to learn how to improve. There were times where it felt so difficult to remain motivated, and it was all too easy to doubt myself. I could not understand why I was continually missing out on job opportunities. I recognise now that I was not in the right frame of mind to grow, or to accept I was making errors in my application. It was this fixed mind-set that I believe hindered my success. When I eventually accepted that I needed to review my approach, and application style, I immediately found an improvement. If you can, take a moment to objectively review the content of your applications and consider these questions:

- Are you making applications to suitable positions?

- Are you using a sensible approach to jobsearches?

- Have you suitably described your experiences to suit different job roles?

- Are you presenting the correct message?

If you have been unsuccessful, do not give up. Take a deep breath, take a break, and carry on. You will get a job!

The next step

Hopefully, your application will be successful and you will be invited for an interview. You will usually receive an email or a phone call from an appointed recruiter (either internal or external) to give you feedback and update you on the next steps of the application process, such as location and format of the interview. You should always use that as an opportunity to learn more about why you were successful and where you can improve. This information can then be leveraged in the interview, but also it can strengthen your other concurrent applications.

Chapter 6: Preparing for interviews

If your job application has been successful and you've been invited for an interview – fantastic! Well done! You've jumped some major hurdles by getting this far, and have beaten several other applicants – maybe even hundreds. There are only a few things left to prepare to impress the hiring managers in the interview. You may be really excited, and want to tell your friends and family. This is fine – even getting an interview is an achievement worth celebrating! – but you should remember that the fight is not over yet, and an interview is never a guarantee of a job offer. More importantly, if you are currently employed, be discreet about who you tell because you never want your manager to find out from hearsay.

Receiving an interview invitation

Most of the time you will receive an interview invitation by phone call from HR, followed up with an email so that you have a formal record of where and when your meeting is. The phone call will allow you to get feedback on your application, but it's also for the recruiter to gauge if you are still interested in the position. It is possible you are having second thoughts and maybe you received another interview offer, so you may be tempted to turn the interview down. However, any hint of your wavering interest will seriously damage your chances of success, so my advice is to maximise your number of opportunities. You may be asked what salary package you are expecting, and what you were most recently on. You don't have to answer this! Basing future salaries on previous earnings is bad practice for companies; they should instead be offering a fair market rate for the role, regardless of the candidate's previous salary. However, that doesn't mean it doesn't happen, and knowing how to respond to such a question takes practice. For this reason, it is prudent to research the typical salary ranges before you apply so you can answer this with confidence. We'll look at this in more detail in Chapter 9.

Avoiding awkward situations

There are a range of potentially awkward situations you may have to navigate during the interview process – but don't panic, preparation is key! Here are a few ideas that may help you:

- If your interview clashes with a client meeting or important work event, ask if you can move the interview to a date that is more suitable. This demonstrates to your interviewer that you value your existing work and client base, which they will respect.

- Virtual interviews are increasingly common, but some companies still prefer face-to-face meetings, so remember to factor in travel times.

- If you have to cancel an interview, do give your interviewer plenty of time to reschedule and have a strong reason. The best way to approach this is to let them know as soon as you can and proactively suggest alternative times and dates.

- You may want to take a full or half day of annual leave on the day of the interview to prepare. Some managers – although they shouldn't! – may ask you why you need the leave, and there are a range of suitable answers that can throw them off the scent. These do not need to be complicated, and the simplest ones are best: you might say you are getting your car fixed, meeting an old friend, or just taking a rest. You could even just say that you have an appointment – after all, this is the truth!

I once had two interviews on the same day, and I arranged them so that one was in the morning and one was in the late afternoon. However, the interview locations were very far away from each other, so I had told each interviewer that I had several urgent meetings that same day. This meant if the first interview over ran, I had a legitimate excuse to draw it a close. Similarly, if I was late to the second interview, I had a legitimate excuse that my earlier meeting over ran. As I've grown more confident, I now realise I could have been honest and said those meetings were interviews.

Read up on the company

Most companies will have "about me" and "news" sections that highlight their core aims, products, services, and achievements. These are great resources of information; detailing product launches, recent business deals or even the locations of their newest offices. Being aware of these minor details shows you are interested in the wider company, and even reading up on the company's latest tweets or social media posts can give you a lot of information really quickly. For example, I found out that one interviewer had recently been to a conference in India, so it was easy to start a rapport with her by asking her about that event. This shows you've taken an active interest in the company and is a real conversation starter.

Expenses

Most companies won't offer travel expenses if there are lots of candidates to interview, across many rounds. However, some organisations do have budget to accommodate specific expenses, so it does not hurt to ask before you attend whether expenses can be covered. This is especially true if you need to travel long distances. An alternative approach is to suggest a video interview for the first round if it is inconvenient to travel. If you are receiving financial support from a job centre, you may be entitled to a reimbursement of expenses relating to work travel.

Interview preparation

Recruiters and hiring managers will check your internet footprint across social media to find out more about you. During one interview, I was asked about how my holiday to Lebanon went: the interviewer had seen my photos and activities on Twitter. This may sound strange, but it is standard practise because companies want to ensure they are hiring reputable staff. You can use this to your advantage by giving a positive impression. For example, if you're applying for a consultancy position in an engineering firm, you can tweet or publish LinkedIn articles on major engineering news stories or industry controversies prior to an interview. This allows you to build a personal brand as someone active in that industry, which can strengthen your position in a job interview. Take time to scan through your public profiles to remove anything you do not want potential employers to see before your interview.

It's the day of the interview, you're nearly there! Don't let up on the planning and prep now – it's showtime.

Making a good impression

Before you even get in the interview room, remember that the interview has begun. Here are some things to be aware of before the meeting starts.

Arriving in person

I never realised how common it is for businesses to share buildings, floors, even office space, with a common reception. The receptionist will usually be aware to expect a visitor, but may not know the exact details such as who you are meeting, especially if they are new or a subcontracted worker. On one occasion, I had three interviews on the same day, but when I arrived for the first meeting, my mind went blank and I completely forgot who I was supposed to be meeting. The receptionist didn't know either and I felt pretty silly. That's why I now always have the key details to hand in a notebook and on my phone.

Some offices, especially those in old city centres with hidden alleyways, aren't obvious to find, especially if you're not a local to that area. I found it really helpful to have a screenshot of the directions I needed, just in case I could not find the details easily in my emails or access the internet. There may be unexpected roadworks which means maps on a search engine won't quite deliver the right directions you need, so be sure to arrive with plenty of time.

Running late

There are almost always delays on the trains in London, but I had no other way of going to and from my interviews. You might not always have the luxury of taking your time or being really early, especially if you look after dependents or have work. The key is to give your interviewer as much warning as possible that you have to be late, or cancel the meeting, and do make sure it is for a good reason. Sadly, I was once stuck on a train that was delayed due to a suicide attempt. I weighed up the options and called HR to let them know about the situation and they were able to accommodate the time change. Luckily, now that remote working and video calls are normal, you might be able to arrange a video interview if travelling is not feasible. However, there is a certain connection with the interviewers you miss out on that you can only get through close interaction.

Dress to impress

An interview is where both sides are selling themselves to the other. Being smartly dressed will leave a positive first impression in your interview, but there are some companies where business attire is more relaxed. If you are in doubt, it is always better to be over-dressed than underdressed, and you don't need expensive clothes to look smart: a clean and polished pair of old shoes look far better than scuffed new ones.

I once worked in an office that dressed casually and I had arranged an interview with another firm during my lunchtime. I didn't want to arouse suspicion by wearing smart clothes to work, but I didn't want to underdress for the interview. I struck a balance, and placed my formal clothes in a small but smart suitcase, and changed prior to the interview in a café nearby. When I arrived at the interview, no one asked why I had a small suitcase, but I was prepared to tell them I was travelling in case they did. I looked great in the interview, no one at work found out, and I got the job!

Match the tone

Most interviews I've attended have started with a friendly tone, but the key is to match the tone of the interviewers, i.e. relax a little if they are relaxed. The hiring manager may introduce you to a few folk before directing you to the interview room, and will usually introduce themselves and the company. At this point I always had my notebook and pen ready to jot down any important information.

Taking notes

Having something to write important details, such as a reliable pen and a notebook, is essential. If you want to type on a tablet or laptop that's fine, but make sure the last app or webpage you used is safe for the work environment, just in case your screen is visible, or the last video you watched is audible. We've all been there!

I developed a particular technique for writing notes during interviews. Before the meeting, I wrote down the key elements of the job, some questions I had, as well as a short description of the interviewers, on the left hand side of a blank double page in my notebook. On the right hand side, I wrote down comments related to those notes during the interview. That way I added structure to what I was writing down and could track if I had any questions that remained unanswered. I also ensured that the next two pages were blank so that I could freely write notes without madly searching for space during the interview.

Introducing yourself

One of the very first things you will likely be asked at the start by the interviewer is to introduce yourself. If you're being interviewed by more than one person, only one may have read your application in depth, so don't assume the interviewers will necessarily remember specific details. In addition, hearing how a person describes themselves out loud can be more informative than reviewing a paper application. Therefore, it is prudent to answer with a full answer, and gauge the level of detail as you proceed.

Just as you tailor your job applications, you should tailor your introduction and personal description to highlight your key skills. For example, mention your excellence in communication if you're applying for a position that requires extensive customer engagement. Short but concise sentences of who you are, what your current role is, and why you want this particular role, are a winning combination.

Confident communication

You should be aiming to speak, present, and act like you would when having a conversation with a friend: confidently, engagingly, and reactively. But don't forget to practice how you communicate verbally and nonverbally. For example, in addition to what you say, you should be mindful of how it sounds. Things like the pace, volume, and natural rhythm of your answer are important. Too fast, and you'll sound nervous; too slow and you'll sound disengaged. If you're worried you are talking too quickly, take a moment to pause to help collect your thoughts. This is especially true if you are presenting as part of the interview. Similarly, how you behave adds detail to your story. Open body language, such as open arms, will help you come across as engaging. Aggressive or defensive body language such as crossed arms, should be avoided. Accidental fidgeting or bad posture will undermine your confidence, so try to stay focused and minimise excessive hand movements. If you are presenting a talk, think about giving equal eye contact to your audience. If all else fails, simply take a deep breath, and smile. That should help you stay calm and positive!

Interviewer tactics

Most of the interviewers I met had a genuine interest in finding out more about me, my motivation, and my interest in the position. However, there are many, many bad interviewers out there. After all – how many people receive training on how to effectively interview before they have to hire their first role? I've met interviewers who played "mind games", and in one particular interview, there was a "good cop" and a "bad cop". The former was calm and polite while the other was aggressive and confrontational. A colleague of mine, who was interviewed by the same people, received a similar treatment. At the time I tried to respond politely and assumed I was being tested to how I respond under pressure. Here are a few other interview tactics I've noticed that you should watch out for:

- **Feigning disinterest:** An interviewer might pretend to lose interest in you or down sell the job role. This is used to gauge your true interest in the position and how you handle a situation where you need to engage with a disinterested person.

- **Random questions:** I was once asked "how much cheese is sold in France each year?" but the answer was not the focus of the question. Rather, the interviewer was gauging my non-verbal reasoning skills and how I handled an unexpected challenge.

- **Being casual:** Watch out when an interviewer says, "relax, this isn't a formal interview" or "we won't judge you." This is a devious tactic designed to bring your guard down and you will definitely be judged on how you respond! On the other hand, an interviewer could genuinely be trying to put you at your ease in an anxious situation – but still, they are there to assess you for the role, so too relaxed is always a bad thing. A corollary of this is the invitation to an "informal chat" which is, in essence, a real interview.

Targeted questions

There is a broad range of potential questions you could be asked but each will be designed to qualify and quantify your competence for the position. Your answers will also determine how well you meet more subjective criteria, such as if you would get along well with your potential colleagues. The interviewers will have some way to score how well you demonstrate that your competencies meet the criteria. Below are a list of targeted questions they may ask to achieve this, as well as ways they are scored, and examples of how to answer with a punch.

- Can you give me an example of when you've had to make effective decisions?

- Can you give me an example of when you've had to communicate effectively?

- Can you give me an example of when you've resolved a conflict?

- Can you give me an example of when you've used your knowledge of the energy sector?

It is so important to practice answering interview questions you might expect so you can maximise your confidence in the interview. It is normal to be nervous before an interview but you can manage your stress by practising your responses, over and over, until they flow naturally like it would in a comfortable conversation you might have with a friend. I have found presenting a balance between comfortable but serious shows I am confident. You can practice with a friend or family member to find the balance that suits you best.

In the written applications, I mentioned that highlighting certain characteristics helps the interviewer pinpoint how your experience makes you an ideal candidate for a specific role. In the interview, a similar approach is needed so that your answer qualifies you have a particular capability and quantifies your proficiency. However, the difference between the written application and the interview is that you have freedom to give more detail because you are not restricted to a word limit. There is, of course, a time restriction. To achieve a balance between detail and time, I use a format to structure my responses to maximise their impact:

- **Situation:** Set the scene where you demonstrated the experience

- **Action:** What did you do in that situation to demonstrate the experience?

- **Result:** What was the outcome of your action?

- **Application:** How will you implement that experience in the new role?

The beauty of this SARA technique is that it allows you to show that you have the experience, quantify your competency, and demonstrate you know how to apply that skill. Below are real questions I've been asked during an interview for a previous position I held, along with the snappy, succinct, but engaging stories I prepared, that answer each well enough:

Can you give me an example of your strength in communication?

"In my current role in sales, I have to pitch to customers frequently to buy my products. This involves phone calls, cold approaches at trade

shows, and presenting at business meetings. When I started, I knew the product well but I didn't always get the right level of interest. I kept at it and honed my pitches, tailoring them more to specific customers' needs. This was much more successful and not only did I sell more products, I also received positive feedback from the customers on how well I presented. I've learned it is important to tailor how you communicate to make the customer feel you care, and I would apply that experience in the role as a technical consultant to give the right information in a way the customer understands."

Can you tell me about your project management experience?

"During my extensive research career I had to manage several lab experiments as part of a series of international collaborations. I achieved this by methodically planning the different projects and when each project milestone had to be reached, accounting for variables such as other lab users and equipment availability, to ensure I met the numerous overlapping deadlines. As I result I was able to complete 5 concurrent projects and write 2 papers. I would use this experience to similarly plan out the different clients I will have to manage as well as when I need to deliver the necessary results for them."

Quantifying Competence

A score card like the one below may be used to qualify and quantify a candidate's skills. You will make the interviewer's job of assessing you much easier by providing them with suitable examples of how you meet the required skills. And they will be grateful!

Required Skill	Competence	High proficiency	Adequate proficiency	Limited proficiency
Essential	Strong communication	✓		
Desirable	Knowledge of the energy sector		✓	

                                    At the interview

More general questions

Below are examples of more general questions that usually crop up to gauge how your personality suits the company's culture. I've suggested how I would answer them; you may like to spend time to come up with your own authentic responses. It's important not to just tweak someone else's answer as your own – not only is it unethical, but that way you will either get found out, or will end up in a job that is not right for you.

Why are you interested in this position/company?

This always comes up at the start of the meeting. Think about why you are passionate for this particular role, will it help you develop a new skill? As for the company, have they achieved success that you want to be part of? You may have heard that the company is the leading business in that sector, or they've just launched a new product. Weaving this into your response helps make your answer more genuine as it shows you have done your research.

What are your strengths/weaknesses?

I used to think it was bad to admit a 'weakness' but now I realise this is asking the candidate to open up on where they think they need further development. Saying you have no weaknesses shows a lack of personal awareness and maturity, while admitting you want to – for example – develop your confidence in public speaking shows you are determined to improve yourself. You should also avoid clichéd fake humility, such as "I work too much". Knowing your strengths should be straightforward, but do think about which strength to highlight in relation to the job role.

What was the last book you read?

I once found myself struggling to come up with the name of even a single book I'd recently read, so I blurted out the last book I studied at school – The Odyssey. I was slightly embarrassed but it led to an interesting conversation about ancient Greece. This question tells the interviewer how rounded an individual you are, so pick something that says a little about your personality and will open up conversation.

Have you applied anywhere else?

This question needs to be handled with tact. It is normal for a candidate to apply to work for a few different companies, in the same way the company will be interviewing lots of candidates. The interviewers will be interested to know where else you have applied as this gauges your interest in the company but also the job role itself. I never volunteered this information, but if I was asked I would answer affirmatively without giving away too much detail. I tried to avoid naming the competitors I've applied to work with, or describing them negatively, so that I could control the conversation's focus back onto why I want to work with the hiring manager I was speaking to. This shows I am an informed, confident candidate, who is in demand. An example I've used includes:

> *"As you might expect, I've had conversations with some of the other key leaders in this field, as I'm really interested in this sector. Even though they've gone well, I feel I have a greater connection with you and that's why I have applied here."*

Have you received any other offers?

I've had interviewers ask whether another company has made me an offer. I've used that to question to my advantage to highlight to the interviewer that I would much rather work with them. You never need to disclose any information about other offers.

> *"I have received a positive offer, but I would rather work with your organisation because ...."*

It is less common for a person to apply for positions in seemingly different fields, but that is often the case for candidates that are moving away from a particular sector. For example, postgraduates transitioning away from academia might be interested in different commercial positions. I applied for a scientific sales position and a recruitment consultancy position around the same time. Both companies were interested to know why I applied to work in two apparently different industries. I argued that my abilities to communicate complicated information and confidence engaging different people, were complementary to both positions. Moreover, both allowed me to develop commercial experience. By explaining my approach, I was able to demonstrate my job applications were actually focused and logical, rather than seemingly scattered. At the same time I reinforced how my skills made me a suitable candidate.

If I made you an offer, would you accept it?

This sounds counter-intuitive, and you would expect that everyone would say yes, but I have heard of a few inexperienced colleagues who truthfully said no. This question is designed to test whether you are truly interested in the role or just want 'any old job'. Even if you do not want the role, and are perhaps holding out for another, saying yes will allow you to maximise your job opportunities. Conversely, saying no will eliminate you from the hiring process. This question lends itself easily to asking what your salary expectations would be. We'll explore this more in Chapter 9 as it more often arises when you are going to be made an offer.

Everybody makes mistakes

In an ideal world, everything would be perfect, but I never appreciated the negative impact that focusing on perfection, rather than progress, can have. Now, I focus on learning from my mistakes, and understanding how to prevent them. It is easier said than done, of course. You may have heard of the failed Mars Orbiter satellite, which disintegrated as it entered the Mars atmosphere. The highly respected defence and aerospace engineering company Lockheed Martin were working with imperial units while the rest of the NASA team used the Metric system. The mistake cost more than $300 million, which could have been avoided through clearer communication. Despite this mistake, Lockheed Martin continues to work on highly specialist and ambitious engineering projects. Yes, mistakes can be costly, but everyone makes them! How you react to them is what is really important. If you slip up, or misspeak during an interview, or if you give the wrong answer in error, that's absolutely fine. Do not beat yourself up about it. Simply address the error (if you think it is worth doing) and move on. If you spend time thinking about your error you will lose concentration and waste time, which will be even more detrimental. Conversely, owning your mistake shows confidence and maturity.

Similarly, if you pause or go blank while answering a question, that is all part of being put under pressure. Obviously it is not ideal, but again, how you react to this says a lot about your personality, which is also being measured. For example, if it is an important question and you answer too quickly but then correct yourself, you may give the impression that you don't take long enough to think about things. However, if you're spending too much time thinking about a straightforward question, there is a danger the interview may overrun. Clearly, there is a balance between taking your time and answering correctly. If you are unsure of the question, it doesn't hurt to hear it repeated. Often, if I need to think about something or remember a detail, I will be direct and I will ask if I can come back to that question. Once I've moved on, I have a little think in the back of my head about the question I missed, and will answer at a suitable point during the interview. This works for me, and you may prefer a different approach. Whatever happens, try to approach each question with confidence and don't let minor slip ups hold you back or distract you.

My story: Unemployment

I was always nervous about admitting that I was unemployed because I was scared this somehow made me an inferior candidate, or that there was something so wrong with me that meant I was not good enough. After many years of reflection,

I recognise that this was a very unhelpful, and even harmful,
attitude, which greatly undermined my mental health. In reality,
I lacked the experience to know that unemployment gaps are
commonplace and that unemployment does not mean you are not
competent. All the hiring managers need is for you to demonstrate
you have the specific skills, experience, and capability to fulfil the
role. Once I realised that I became much more confident.

Remember, if you've been invited to an interview, this means
that the hiring manager likes you and that they have seen your
potential, rather than what you lack! An interviewer is too busy
to meet people who aren't viable candidates, so stay positive!
For example, unemployment taught me how to be resilient
despite numerous unsuccessful job applications. I would also
say something like that if I was asked about my unemployment
gap, as it's an admirable skill for any job. Remember to shift the
conversation onto your positive attributes.

Your questions

A good sign of a free flowing conversation is that both sides are asking
questions. Asking specific questions shows you've been paying attention
and reinforces your interest in the position. You should be able to come
up with a few questions throughout the interview and any notes you've
written might inspire you. I often found that a lot of the questions I wanted
to ask were answered naturally during the interviews and I made a note
of the answers so that I could easily refer to them later on to help me
decide how I felt about the role.

Occasionally, there might be very little information in the job description,
especially if the role is new. The job I eventually accepted after my period
of unemployment did not have a detailed job description at all and I had
to piece together what the role involved from information I gathered in
the interview. The basic job description meant there was lots of flexibility
in the role. However, at times I was unsure if certain responsibilities were
expected or beyond the remit of the role, nor was the career progression
pathway obvious. Lack of clarity about any facet of the job will introduce
confusion later on. This is a key example of why asking the right questions
about the role is really important. Your questions are the best opportunity
you have of asking the hiring manager to clarify the expected duties.
Below are a few good stock questions to ask if you are unsure what to ask:

How do you measure your company's / employees' performance?

By asking about how the company monitors its success, and hence how it maintains its income, you demonstrate a genuine interest in the company itself. Similarly, an awareness that monitoring performance is important shows you understand that is a critical part of the job. The answer will usually be a key performance indicator (KPI) such as the number of products sold or services delivered, per month or year. The answer may also reveal the company's revenue model and how much of a role commission contributes to an employee's salary.

What's your most successful project?

This is a good question to ask if you want to know about the highs and lows of the position. Is there a high-stress/high-reward attitude? How passionate are the other employees? How often might you get to be proud of your achievements there?

Who are your main competitors?

This sounds awkward but it really isn't because being aware of the competition shows commercial maturity. Some interviewers might expect you to know exactly who the main competitors are, especially if you are applying to work for a well-known company. However, if you are interviewing with a small or really specialised company, in a niche field, the competitors might not be so obvious. During one meeting, my interviewers named their competitor and I was able to research that company before the next interview. I noticed that both companies visited the same trade shows and targeted similar customers, but only the competitor made regular presentations at those shows. I used this knowledge to suggest a new marketing approach during my second interview, and the hiring manager was impressed at my proactive research.

Can I meet some of your colleagues?

It is best to ask this after you've had your first interview because you will have already established a rapport with the interviewer. Meeting the co-workers will tell you lots about whether you will enjoy working there, or if there are any office politics. The colleagues will tell you about things like job perks, benefits, and if you get nice new gadgets or have to use old furniture. You can also get an insight into how laid back the staff are, or if people have a long lunchbreak rather than a quick 30 minutes eating at their desks. However, be aware that this is still part of the interview, and your behaviour will form part of the hiring manager's decision.

Have you seen many other candidates?

Think of this as the reverse of the question they might ask you about where else you are interviewing. This tells you how sought after the position is. Many candidates will mean it is a highly competitive process, but if there have been only a few candidates, maybe the interviewers are looking for a particular type of candidate. This question also reminds your interviewers that you are aware of how interviews work. They're interviewing you but you are also interviewing them.

Discrimination

It is a sad fact of working life that some employees, but also job applicants, will face some form of either intentional or inadvertent discrimination. Discrimination legislation is designed to protect employees, but also job applicants, throughout their employment lifecycle. This includes the application process, right through to employment, and eventual termination of the working contract. Unfair treatment may include indirect discrimination, if a candidate is treated differently based on who they are perceived to be associated with.

Discrimination involves prejudicial treatment of a person perceived to have one or several protected characteristics, such as age, sex, or race. In many parts of the world these may include: disability; gender reassignment status; marriage and civil partnership; pregnancy and maternity; religion or belief; and sexual orientation. Discrimination can appear in many forms, such as an inappropriate question, unequal treatment, or absence of reasonable adjustment.

Inappropriate questions

I was speaking to a colleague of mine about negative experiences at interviews. He was asked if he was going to have more children, because the interviewer wanted to be mindful of an absence due to paternity leave. Making a hiring decision based on the answers about protected statuses is discrimination and such a question is not acceptable during an interview. I was once asked whether my name was African or Turkish. My instinct was to respond sharply, but in the heat of the moment, I brushed the question away as I did not want to appear rude. It can be so difficult to navigate inappropriate behaviour, but if you feel you are being asked a question that sounds unsuitable, you can ask calmly how the question relates to how you fulfil the role. You could try saying something like "Oh! Why do you ask?" or "I'm not quite sure what you're getting at, here – could you elaborate on what you're hoping to ascertain from my answer?".

Reasonable adjustments or accommodations

In the UK, the employer is required to make reasonable adjustments to overcome any disadvantage a disabled person might have compared to an able-bodied person. This adjustment spans the entire recruitment process including advertising the role, the application process, shortlisting candidates, the interview, as well as employment (such as onboarding). The latter may be particularly important if you have become disabled during a period of employment. Crucially, a candidate is entitled to reasonable adjustments without the need to disclose the specific nature of the disability. Reasonable adjustments may include extra time to complete performance assessments, or more accessible instructions. Other reasonable adjustments include providing specialist software, or providing time off for specific appointments. Do try to give the employer sufficient time to arrange the reasonable adjustments. Even though you do not need to disclose your disability, you may choose to.

Some companies are shifting to skills-based assessments of candidates, which focuses on their abilities, rather than which university they went to, as the latter can lead to socio-economic discrimination. While I am very much in favour of this approach, this is by far not a standard approach yet. Hopefully your whole job application experience is free of discrimination, but if you feel that you have experienced any unfair treatment, you should keep a written record of the incident so that you can refer back to it later. You should also consider making a formal complaint in writing to the HR department. For more information about this topic, you can try contacting employment charities, workers' unions and citizens' advice bureaus, as well as job centres, most of whom will offer free advice or direct you to further information. If you want to know if a company has a policy on discrimination, you can search its website, or ask HR.

Before you go

A strong introduction helps you set the tone of the interview, and a strong outro will help you end the meeting on a high note. A formula that works well for me is to: thank the interviewers for their time; remind them why I am excited about the position; summarise my key strengths; and mention how they make me suitable for the position. Find the structure that works well for you, but try to keep it simple and snappy. This makes it easier for the interviewers to remember you when they write up their notes on how you interviewed. Ideally, you can reference any key points you discussed.

Chapter 8:
After the interview

A really good habit I have learnt over the years is to write up the key points and outstanding actions following a meeting, as soon as possible. This allows you to focus on the important details, and identify the next steps to progress the meeting. The same is true for an interview – which, after all, is simply another kind of business meeting. This does not mean you need to write down everything, but you should jot down any questions you answered well, areas you could do better on, and important details about the job you learnt, as well as any follow-up actions you need to do. This will serve as a good record of what happened and will help you tailor your response to the interviewer.

Follow up

Try to send your follow up response within 24 hours of your meeting, thanking the interviewers for their time and for the opportunity to learn more about the role. Where you can flourish and really stand out is by referencing some detail you discussed in the meeting; this shows you have really thought about your conversation. Maybe you could add an insightful and relevant fact you learned, or elaborate on a topic you discussed. Try to keep your response concise, with no more than 5-6 sentences. Some organisations require you to direct your replies to HR rather than the interviewer, but the content will be passed on.

You should receive feedback on your interview and the next steps of the application process by email. However, you may also receive a telephone call, especially if you've worked with a recruiter. Having a written record of your interview will help you quickly remember the key points of the meeting, so you maximise the discussion on the phone. If your interview went well, many congratulations! We'll delve into how to handle positive feedback and progress with job offers in the next few chapters. If you have been unsuccessful, don't lose heart; you have achieved a great deal thus far. Instead of beating yourself up, focus on what you did well and how you can improve. Below is an overview of how I handled some unsuccessful interviews over the past few years.

Learnings from unsuccessful interviews

Below are three memorable, but unsuccessful interviews I've had, as well as what I learned about my own development. In all cases, I tried to handle the feedback with maturity and grace. I thanked the interviewer for their time and tried to factor in their comments so that I would not make the same mistake again.

Sales manager for an instrument manufacturer

I had worked hard to get an interview, which involved regular follow ups with the HR manager because the position had been initially been filled, but was later re-opened. I presented a pitch of their own product to the interviewers to demonstrate my technical and sales experience, which went down well. However, where I fell short was that I asked for too high a salary and benefit package for my experience level. The HR manager told me this directly by phone after the interview and I recognise she was right. I should have carried out a little more research on the salaries in that field and compared them to my experience level.

Consultant for executive search

I alluded to this bittersweet moment at the start of this book. This was my first interview outside of academia; I'd stumbled upon it from sheer dumb luck, by finding myself sat next to the hiring manager on a flight. I went into the interview with such a high opinion of myself, based on nothing more than the fact I was intelligent. I remember saying in the interview that I expected to be a senior consultant as I had a PhD. Rather ironically, for someone so smart, I was pretty ignorant of how the world of business operates: experience and capability is usually valued more highly than level of education. The interviewer called me a day after our meeting to let me know that I had been unsuccessful because he did not feel there was a good enough culture fit. At the time, I was confused because I had aced the administrative task he had set me. I now see that I did not have the right attitude for the position, and that is just as important as smarts.

Research associate in a university spin-out

In the earliest days of my job hunt, I was still exploring technical positions. I received an interview, along with three others out of 95 other candidates. Although I was so enthusiastic about the position, I had not prepared sufficiently for the interview. I was overly confident and made some basic errors when I was asked about my experience. I had not reminded myself of what I had written in my application, and couldn't remember which specific examples I had put in my CV. I was able to answer the questions eventually, but I could have given a stronger response had I read through my application and reminded myself of the role's requirements.

All of these experiences have helped me become a better candidate, both in the interview but also at work. Each working day is essentially an interview; you are being assessed for behaviour and capability. People who do well are promoted, and those who are not are given feedback to develop. If there is one unifying message all those experiences tell me, it's that I need to work on how I come across, and manage my expectations. And I have come a long way from who I used to be. You may find that there are other character and skill traits you need to work on. Feedback is how you identify the strengths you should highlight and the areas that need more attention. No matter what feedback you receive after an interview, remember to focus on the positives: we are all learning all the time. Being invited for an interview is a great achievement, and if you've got one interview invitation, there is no reason why you can't get another!

If you decide to reapply for the same position if it opens up again, you can use the feedback you received from your initial application to improve your resubmission, and show the interviewer that you are receptive to personal development.

A proactive approach saves the day

One cold, autumnal morning, I was standing on a wet station platform, waiting for yet another delayed train. My phone buzzed with an email alert – my job application for a laboratory supervisor in a plastics factory had been unsuccessful. I was distraught. I really felt that I was well suited to that role, and it was exactly what I wanted: a commercial role within a scientific environment. On the journey home I had thought about where I had gone wrong because the email contained no feedback. After planning out my approach, I called the HR manager to ask for that feedback but also express my disappointment. She was pleasantly surprised to receive my call. She mentioned that I

Proactivity

I once got a call from a recruiter late on a Wednesday night and she invited me to meet her at her office at 8:30 the next morning. Before she hung up the phone, she promised to send me a follow up email and her office address. Unfortunately, those details never came through and I suspect she may have misheard my email address. Luckily, I had written down her name and the company's office, which meant it was easy to search for the address. Despite not receiving any directions, I was still able to meet her the next day, which earned me a lot of positive recognition. Recruitment teams love it when candidates show initiative!

lacked the experience necessary for the position, but she then mentioned that her colleague in a related industry was looking to hire someone with a similar profile to me. In fact, she was so impressed with my attitude and that I had taken the initiative to ask for feedback directly, she referred me to her contact. I was overjoyed! I almost fell off my chair in my scramble to follow up on this new opportunity. One month, and two interviews later I was offered the job, which I accepted with jubilation. It really goes to show that being proactive can be beneficial for you, and it impresses your interviewers. I used to think that getting a job like this was somehow inferior and that relying on a mutual connection rather than merit alone was shameful. It could not be further from the truth. People trust their contacts and a good recommendation can go further than what grade you received in your school or college.

Section 3:
The transition

How to handle job offers, manage the resignation process, and start a new role off on the right foot.

Chapter 9:
Receiving a job offer

One day – hopefully soon! – you will be the happy recipient of a job offer. The interviewer may wish to make you an offer face-to-face in the meeting, or shortly after the interview by phone if they need time to discuss it internally. In the moment between receiving an offer and accepting (or rejecting) it, you will have the upper hand. Will you negotiate a better work package, or will you use the offer to leverage a better salary at your existing workplace? Before we explore how to handle the different negotiating conditions, we need to understand what the aim of negotiation is, and what is open for negotiation. We'll also cover why it is important to receive a formal offer in writing and to take time to reflect on a job offer.

The purpose of a negotiation is to find a mutually beneficial set of working conditions for both parties. Some conditions may be fixed, such as the termination policy, while others can be negotiable, such as pay. In most companies, before an employee is hired there will have been agreed a budget as part of a business plan. This budget will dictate how many employees can be hired, and at what pay band, across a certain time period. For almost all businesses of any size, this is a rigid structure that limits how much, and how often, employees can be hired and promoted. Although there is some flexibility in the pay band, there will always be an upper limit. If you can research what that is, you can use that to your advantage. However, it's not just salary that you need to consider: your final offer will usually include other employee benefits, which may or may not be negotiable too. You can use the interview to determine what these benefits are, and how flexible the company is on what they offer.

Base pay and working conditions

If you are transitioning from one sector to another, you may not always enter at the same level of seniority or pay as you started with. When I left academia to join the commercial sector I dropped roughly £3k in my annual salary, but this is something I was expecting based on my research of the employment conditions in the sector I was interested in – try to be aware of realistic pay ranges for the positions you are targeting. In my case, although I did have to take that small pay cut, I was also able to negotiate a reduction in the probation period from three months to one. This gave me quicker access to other perks, such as a more lucrative pension plan, which for me made up for the reduction in take-home pay.

Bonuses

These are taxable benefits that may be paid regularly or annually, and are usually dependent on performance. The frequency and quantity of a bonus will usually depend on job type. They may be discretionary for entry level positions, while senior managers may negotiate a bonus as a contractual obligation.

Holidays

While public sector jobs tend to offer lower salaries than the private sector, they may offer better holiday packages. Some companies even allow you to sell back unused holidays for cash, or buy them if you need more. Is that something that is important to you?

Flexible working

Smaller companies may not always be able to afford to pay higher salaries than larger corporate companies, but they may allow you to work more flexible hours, reduced hours, or from home. You may be interested in negotiating a later starting date to give you time to move jobs.

Parental benefits

The statutory parental leave varies by country, but what is considered 'normal' also varies by industry. Consider too if there is an employee discount on nearby childcare facilities, or you can always ask if they are open to providing one. Some companies offer in-house childcare, and some will offer shared parental leave.

Your job title

In industries which have a clear path of progression, such as consultant, senior consultant, and principal consultant, there won't be much leeway to change your title. However, other industries, and small companies, are flexible to requests for a change in employee title. This may not carry any immediate financial benefit, but it can make your CV look more attractive for a future move.

Professional & personal development

Companies will look to support employee development in a range of methods, which can open multiple avenues for discussion: can you expense membership to a professional industry body? Is there a budget for employee training that the company will pay for? Do they recognise a trade union? Is there an opportunity to lead a team or develop a product?

Tax breaks

Some companies allow you to pay less income tax by offering benefits such as season ticket loans, or pension payments. For entry level positions, this might give you back enough to pay for a few meals with your friends every month.

Other perks

If you typically buy a coffee every day, how much could you save a year if your work paid for free coffees? Or do you prefer fresh fruit or gym access? Maybe access to private dental and health care is what you are looking for? Find out if there are any other perks that are free, or offered at a reduced rate, such as a company car, that might otherwise be an expense.

All of the above add up to make up your final pay package. Before you can negotiate, you need to know what is being offered in total and how that compares to what you're getting now, and what the average offering is across different industries. Do your own research, and calculate your needs with a budget and a good idea of your expenditure and habits in order to be able to properly consider an offer. Ideally, you'll do this research before you apply, so that you can go into the interview, and any calls with HR, well informed.

How to approach the negotiation

Before you enter the interview, you may have already been asked what salary you currently earn and what you are expecting. Although it can be uncomfortable, I try to avoid giving a direct answer to these questions, because I do not want to set any conditions before I have better understood the role. Especially about your current salary – pay should be based on what the role is worth, not what the person holding it previously earned. Of course, this won't stop a lot of employers asking! This is why it is prudent to research the typical salary ranges before you apply, so you can enter this discussion with confidence. Ideally, you will try and direct the conversation back to a suitable range for the role, based on what you know so far. In answer to direct questions about your salary, you could say something like: "I prefer not to disclose my current situation, but I am happy to confirm that my expectations are within the advertised range for this role." Or perhaps they haven't advertised a salary at all – when questioned on your expectations, you might say: "I have of course looked into market rates for this role, but I was hoping that you would be able to provide me with a ballpark range?"

Sometimes, you won't be able to avoid giving a numerical answer – standing your ground must always be balanced with not being so difficult that you're out of the running. This takes practice, so you should research the typical pay range for the given industry and location, you're seeking to enter, which you can use as a guide to suggest a suitable salary. Your answer will be noted, so that the interviewer can leverage that in any negotiation, which will usually happen towards the end of the final interview, or after an offer is received.

Talking money

Approach the topic of salary, benefits and remuneration with confidence and maturity. Negotiations are not demands, they are queries. Both parties are trying to find out how to reach a happy middle ground, so try to view the process as two parties looking to solve a mutual challenge, rather than a tussle. You may be asked to suggest your preferred salary, or one may be suggested by the interviewer.

Modern negotiation advice tells us to avoid making the first move if possible, as this will anchor the conversation around that offer. For example, if you suggest £40k as a starting point, the counter offer you will receive will typically be lower than this, not higher. Where as if they started at £40k, you can counter with a higher, rather than lower proposition. Other commonly touted tips advise suggesting a specific number, such as £39,700, rather than a whole number, because this implies you have thoroughly calculated what you need for the position. I personally think this is too gimmicky and is not suitable for the types of the positions I apply for.

It can be tricky to avoid going first, as you may think it is rude or there may be an awkward silence you want to fill. These are all part of the negotiation experience, and the more you practice this 'awkwardness' the easier you will find it. If your offer is lower than they expected they may agree to your offer, and you may leave thinking you could have gone higher! If you've suggested a starting point that is too high, the interviewer will then likely make a lower counter offer, £35k, say. You then have the opportunity to negotiate. Say something along the lines of "is there any scope for improvement regarding salary?" There is no need to justify this suggestion, but if you feel compelled to, you can use positive feedback you've received to remind the interviewer of your strengths. For example, "the skills I will be employing are commensurate with a higher salary in this industry." You can then use the positive feedback you received to leverage that higher salary. You can in principle use another job offer as a bargaining chip, and I've done this to receive an improved offer of £4k for a former role. However, this strategy can be risky if you do not actually have another offer to fall back on, so be prepared for them to call you out on this.

If you have negotiated something that deviates from a pre-approved guideline, they may need to review that with their manager. They will then come back and decline your request (and insist on their best offer) or accept it. Keep a written record of the final offer, especially if you negotiated something specific. This will be useful when you review the contract if you accept the offer.

Whatever the outcome of the negotiation, do explore improving your working conditions. Negotiations are anticipated, especially for commercial positions. The specific package will be dependent on the company's annual performance, but also external factors such as political or economy uncertainty. This is why researching the market will help you be prepared. Finally, avoid justifying a higher salary based on emotions, such as anger or upset. Negotiations are agreed by reasoning a strong commercial argument, and how you add value. Remember, negotiating is about problem solving and is a skill that gets easier, the more you practice. Why not take turns role playing with a friend as part of an interview preparation?

Negotiation 1

Negotiations occur in everyday conversations, from the high pressures of the board room, through to more mundane upselling of biscuits in a coffee shop. Learning how to detect and react to negotiations is a helpful life skill. I've had two really good books recommended to me by sales manager colleagues that serve as a good source of further information: Never Split the Difference by Voss & Raz provides general insight to situational negotiation, while Negotiation Genius by Malhotra & Bazerman provides more detail on the theory behind negotiation.

Taking time

Once an offer has been made, and a salary negotiated and agreed, the next step is to ask for some time to think about the offer. There is no requirement to accept it on the spot, and you won't be asked why you need time. Any employer who tries to pressure you to accept on the spot is showing concerning red flags, as it is perfectly normal to discuss offers after an interview, or to take something away to consider it. If you're certain you want the job then you might want to sign a contract immediately. However, you might be waiting to hear back from your other interviews to weight up multiple offers. Asking for a few days or over the weekend is reasonable, but a week is not unheard of. You may have personal decisions that you need to discuss with a spouse or dependant.

Taking time will allow you to make a decision based on reason rather than emotion. If you decide to accept the offer, in most cases you will then receive a contract, which you should review thoroughly. The major exception here is in the US, where employment contracts are not the norm. They're still not unheard of though, so if you are asked to sign one, make sure you read and understand it! There will be lots of standard terms and conditions, but pay close attention to anything you have negotiated such as number of working days, office location, salary, and bonus, as well as resignation conditions. If there are any discrepancies between what you have read and what you agreed in the interview, make sure to get further clarity before you sign.

Making a choice

Towards the end of my unemployment, I had received offers from two executive search firms in the City of London, and a marketing position offer for a tech company in the suburbs. All offered similar base salaries, but the City jobs offered far greater bonus opportunities. I reviewed the companies' online profiles and employee reviews, and the impression I got was that the City companies embodied a cutthroat attitude and long working hours, which I suppose I expected. By contrast, the marketing position was for a larger company that specialised in selling scientific equipment in a friendly environment, which was much more aligned with my strengths and background. This meant that despite the lower take home pay, I felt I would perform better, and be happier in the marketing role. From speaking to other working professionals within my network over the years, I recognise that salary is not the only driver for making job decisions. Of course it is important, but there are so many other factors that may influence you on a personal level. These include the company's reputation, attitudes to sustainability, record of employee happiness, or even geographical location. If you are fortunate to receive multiple job offers, I found these questions helped me determine which would make me happiest:

- Which company did I prefer before the job offers?

- Which company will give me the most opportunities to develop?

- What kind of person can I become after working at each position?

- Which working environment will I thrive in?

- Which will make me happy to leap out of bed in the morning?

After a few days of mulling over my job offers, I made a decision to accept the marketing role based on what felt best to me. I called the company to confirm and signed the contract that same day after a thorough read through. I sent the email off, with a request for a read-receipt. I waited eagerly for the company to countersign the contract. I felt so giddy and had a grin as wide as the Grand Canyon; I was simply ecstatic. When I finally received the countersigned contract I breathed a sigh of relief, and went to bed. I had the best sleep in over a year, and all I could think about for the next month was one thing. I finally had a job! In recent years when I have moved on from one job to another, that sense of joy and relief remains, but there are a few things to consider before you officially accept or decline an offer.

Managing the offers

Sharing the joys of a job offer with family and friends can be cathartic but do take care to manage your expectations. Job offers are conditional, and nothing is confirmed until you have a signed contract. A close friend received an offer for a senior management position, but the company went through financial trouble and the hiring budget was temporarily frozen. He had to wait 6 months until the budget was released for the company to send through the contract. This is an extreme example of why you should not publicise any offer until you sign a contract. Not only can it cause you embarrassment if it falls through, if you are currently employed there is a danger your manager can find out which could become a difficult situation. More common reasons for delays in your contract being processed could be from HR personnel on leave or the fact that companies (especially European ones) take long holidays in summer.

Similarly, if you have multiple offers, try not to decline any until you have a signed contract for the job you prefer. When I came to decline the two City job offers, I received very different reactions. I got on far better with one manager, and she was very graceful in thanking me for my time and reminding me what she enjoyed about my profile. She even took the time to call me to receive feedback on how she could improve. It was strange to hear her ask this and it reminded me of the many emails that I had sent, pleading for feedback. Conversely, when the manager for the other position called me, he was keen to change my mind and offered a small increase in base salary. When I politely, but confidently, declined this offer, he called back three days later and tried the same approach again. He then told me that if I ever reconsidered, I would be welcome to contact him again.

Declining an offer can feel strange, as it is usually a rare occurrence early in the career ladder. As with all communication with your interviewers, you should remain professional, even if you know for certain that you don't want a particular position. You can never tell when you will next see that hiring manager again, and you always want to leave a good impression. As I've grown, I've learnt to build and maintain relationships, which helps create, rather than close opportunities. For this reason, I try to maintain connections I have made, including hiring managers I know. When I decline an offer I thank them for their time but also let them know that I will keep an eye out for suitable candidates that might be interested in similar positions. This involves minimal effort on my part, but opens an avenue for future dialogue.

Making your choice

You can use social media as a window into the behaviour, finances, as well as social and environmental impact of companies you've applied to. For example, sites like Glassdoor allow employees to rate their companies so you can read what the operations team really think, learn what perks the sales department get, as well as determine if there is a high turnover of graduate employees or not. This is useful ammunition to help you decide how you feel about a certain company or position.

Chapter 10: Nearing the finish line

That transient period between accepting a job, and actually starting, is short lived. It's now time to relax, celebrate, and address a few final affairs.

Resigning your current job

Resigning can be daunting because you need to find the right time and place, which can be difficult in a busy office – and trickier still if you work from home. If possible, try to book a meeting in your manager's diary with a fairly generic title, such as "progress update." You may be asked why you wish to resign, and you do not have to specify any reasons, but it helps to be prepared to answer this question. You should ask if there are any specific procedures you need to go through. Handling the resignation with grace will help you maintain a good working relationship with your manager and with the company, which could create a future opportunity for you. Do take the opportunity to ask if there is any feedback you can get to continue your development.

Normally, you will need to send a formal letter to HR, but some organisations may require you to delete confidential information or return your security pass, for example. HR may invite you to an exit interview, so they can record your feedback to help improve how the business functions. It can be tempting to say how you honestly feel (especially if you have had a poor working experience) but I have tried to avoid oversharing anything too personal. My experience is that if a situation can get to be toxic in an organisation, HR will generally not care enough what you have to say once you leave. But I hope that is not the case where you work.

Letting other people know

You may have worked with another team member or external client and developed a strong connection. Consider giving them a courtesy email to let them know. Better still would be a call or in-person meeting as this will help maintain that relationship should you need to engage with them in future. Some companies have clauses in the contract that stipulate how you can and cannot engage with a former contact once you have left the organisation, so be sure to check your contract.

If you have worked with recruiters, whether successfully or otherwise, do let them know you are no longer in need of their services. While it is not strictly necessary to do this, it does help you retain a professional working relationship, which is useful, especially if you need their help in the near future. You may also wish to update any online job profiles so that recruiters no longer consider you for opportunities.

Financial planning

A new job will mean a change in financial situation, whether positive or negative. Consider when the change will be noticed, and by how much, so you can better plan for the regular expenses, such as rent, bills, or child care. If your new working environment requires you to relocate, take the time to plan ahead how much a move would cost. If you've sought financial assistance from a job centre, you may be required to update them of your new employment status. You may be able to receive continued support such as discount travel, but this is highly specific to each region, so be sure to find out what you are entitled to.

Home

Use the time to explore if you need new or more suitable work clothes or equipment. It is time to physically (and emotionally) declutter. If you have time between jobs, take the opportunity to get into an exercise regime, or other healthy habit you want to cultivate. By starting a schedule before you start a new job, you will be more inclined to stick to it. Exercise can do wonders for your physical and mental health. Small, steady steps of progress are more manageable and achievable than large, overly ambitious goals.

Preparing for the new role

Try to read up on any relevant information, such as the company's activity or news from the wider industry. This will help you to start conversations with the new colleagues you will meet. In the first few days of a new role, you will still need to familiarise yourself with your surroundings and the responsibilities, so don't expect too much of yourself. You may receive an employee handbook full of company policies, as well as an overview of the organisation and its key departments. Take time to understand how the company functions and who the team leaders that you will be engaging with are. This will make sure you get to know the right people early on, which will help you get off to a flying start. During my jobsearch, I learnt how to bake bread and cakes, and I found it cathartic to continue doing that in my spare time after work. It meant that I became confident enough to share my bakes with my new team, which was a great ice-breaker and a quick way to raise my profile. Do you have a hobby that is exciting to share?

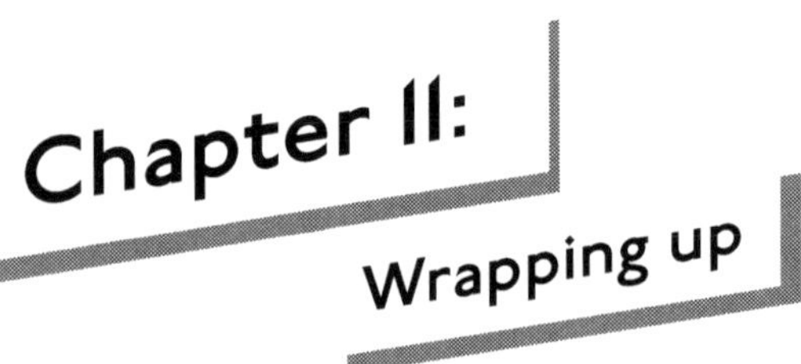

Chapter 11:
Wrapping up

I hope you've enjoyed reading this book and found the insights to employment secrets helpful. Fundamental to increasing your employability is recognising how adaptable you are. To do that, it is key to explore where your strengths lie, where you need to develop, and to understand what motivates you. No matter where you are on your employment journey, consider these core messages of personal growth and positive mental health attitudes, to help you navigate your own career path:

- Add structure to your day, through exercise or activities that help you learn and grow. Set small achievable, realistic goals – this is especially important if you have limited time

- Everyone needs assistance at some point in their life and career. Don't be afraid to reach out to your wider network for knowledge or guidance, or professional financial and mental health support if you need it

- Everyone makes mistakes when they are learning something new. There is no shame in not succeeding; focus instead on learning from past mistakes in order to grow

- Everyone is on their own career path, facing their own challenges. Comparisons with their achievements can be unhealthy. Instead, look to measure your own achievements by comparing where you are now to where you used to be.

- Maintain relationships with your network as these will help create opportunities in the short and long term

- Search for constructive feedback to develop your capabilities, strengthen your applications, and give you confidence in job applications and interviews

My story: What I did next

It took me a long time to really appreciate the impact that both
the jobsearch experience and my subsequent employment had
had on my mental health. I was fortunate enough to come across
valuable resources (both people and books) which opened my
eyes to the value of self-reflection and mental growth. The more
I learned about who I was, what I liked, and what I didn't, the
more comfortable I became with my situation. That acceptance
eased the mental pressure of guilt and shame that I had burdened
myself with. It is ok to be unemployed, it is ok to need help, and it
is ok fall down. In my quest to get back up on my feet, I recognised
that there were so few sources of engaging and modern career
guidance, based on first-hand experiences, relevant to people
like me: highly-educated but inexperienced early-to-mid career
professionals. This is why I wrote this book, to provide that
much needed guidance on employability but also mental health.
Over the past few years I have volunteered my time to present
at career seminars the lessons I've learned, and to give back
to a community I am so keen to support — early-to-mid career
jobseekers. I have noticed there is a continual need for knowledge
transfer on employability, as well as guidance on how to progress
in a role, and climb the career ladder. For this reason I have set
up a company to help professionals improve their confidence and
communication, to further their career. I am also in the process
of developing a book on career progression based on first hand
experiences.

I hope you have enjoyed the practical templates and highlighted Key
Points that will help you action the career advice and land your next
dream job. I would love to hear your story, and learn about your career
challenges – reach me on Twitter at **@fawzi_ac** or at my website **www.
chahineiet.com**, to discuss any of the points raised, or to get career advice
suited to your needs.

I wish you the best of luck in your jobsearch. Remember to stay positive!

Thanks

I have to thank a lot of people who have helped me in developing this book and myself.

First and foremost, my thanks go to several dear friends: Ana Belen Jorge Sobrido, Ellen Barker, Oleg Glebov, and William Campbell. Each of you has given support in the way that you can, be it friendship, time, optimism, or wine. We have enjoyed both the highs and lows, the laughs and tears.

I must thank TJ Preston and Alejandro Tomassi for challenging me and always providing an alternative, objective perspective, without which I would not have grown, both professionally and mentally. I am the person I am today because of the conversations we have had. I am also grateful to Léa Decours, Marios Hatzopoulos, and Joe Renney for your insights into the inner workings of different industries which helped ground the book.

I have had the fortune to work with Rebecca Bush, an eagled-eyed editor with an acerbic wit. Your gift is to transform words and ideas into exact meaning. To my designer, and friend, Kathryn Corlett, your artistic talent has been invaluable in adding the depth this book needed. I am also indebted to the kind and generous support raised by the Kickstarter community, comprising good friends and generous strangers, who believed in this social project to create fresh and engaging career advice. Without you this project could not have happened.

Lastly, I will always be grateful for the patience, love and care my family have shown over the years and more recently. You have all been supportive in your own way and I am immensely proud of, and inspired by, what you have achieved. You have shown me that success can come in all forms, and that few things matter more than happiness. Thank you.

About the author

Fawzi Abou-Chahine PhD is the director of Chahine Communications, where he helps innovative companies articulate their research to secure funding. He devotes part of his time coaching technical staff and postgraduate researchers to communicate their work more confidently, and find rewarding careers. Over the years he has helped companies fund their innovation through writing commercial bids as a business development lead at NPL, and technical reports as a consultant at Leyton. Prior to establishing a commercial career, he held research positions in Finland on solar cell materials, a PhD scholarship in Bristol on chemical physics, and a Master's degree from UCL where he researched hydrogen storage technology.

Made in the USA
Columbia, SC
16 December 2022

74116526R00052